WHEN I WAS A CHILD...

A Journey From Religion To Relationship

By

George R. Montgomery, Sr.

Copyright © 2024 by George R. Montgomery, Sr.

All rights reserved. This book or any portion thereof may not be reproduced or used in any manner whatsoever without the express written permission of the publisher except for the use of brief quotations in a book review.

Printed in the United States of America

First Edition, 2024

HARDBACK ISBN: 979-8-8692-2190-2

PAPERBACK ISBN: 979-8-8692-2187-2

EBOOK ISBN: 979-8-8692-2188-9

Red Pen Edits and Consulting

www.redpeneditsllc.com

Some journeys have an ending, a destination point.
Some journeys are lifelong pursuits.
My journey is still in progress…

      GEORGE R. MONTGOMERY, SR.

"It would be a sad thing to die and leave behind the book that God placed inside of you – no one would ever hear your story because you were too afraid to write it."

      PASTOR CHARLES JACOB
      NEXT LEVEL MINISTRIES
      CHARLOTTE, NC

CONTENTS

Acknowledgments And Dedications   1

Foreword   3

Introduction   6

CHAPTER 1
    In The Beginning   11

CHAPTER 2
    When I Was A Child   19

CHAPTER 3
    A Good Soldier   27

CHAPTER 4
    The Glory Of The First House   33

CHAPTER 5
    The Essence Of Tradition   43

CHAPTER 6
    Expanding My Horizon   55

CHAPTER 7
    The Awakening   61

CHAPTER 8
Delivered From Denominations — 71

CHAPTER 9
I Hear Trumpets! — 81

CHAPTER 10
The Silent Killer — 95

CHAPTER 11
The Man In The Mirror — 101

CHAPTER 12
Following The Cloud — 111

CHAPTER 13
School Is Now In Session — 119

CHAPTER 14
A Recipe For Disaster — 125

CHAPTER 15
The Science Of Hoop-A-Letics — 131

CHAPTER 16
Discovering Worship — 137

CHAPTER 17
Shifting To A New Paradigm — 147

CHAPTER 18
    Anointed For Purpose   155

CHAPTER 19
    Where Healing Begins   163

CHAPTER 20
    The Enemies Of Purpose   183

About The Author   198

ACKNOWLEDGMENTS AND DEDICATIONS

There are so many individuals who have played a significant role in my life as I have grown up from a child to adulthood. I have had countless people pour into my life words of encouragement, life-impacting decision-making, a shoulder to lean on and cry on when needed, and timely and significant support when there was a need. For those of you, and you know who you are, I acknowledge, and I am indebted and thankful to you.

At the core of my being, I know that without my wife, Elleanor, and our three adults, Keosha, Courtney, and George, Jr., I would not have made it this far.

You all have seen me at the lowest points of my life and still loved and cared for me.

You all have been there when no one else was there. At times when I could not carry myself, you stepped in and placed me on your shoulders, and collectively carried me.

Thank you, Elleanor for loving me, carrying me, praying for me, and fighting for me, for 41 years. You have been faithful and trustworthy when it came to protecting me at my most vulnerable times. To my eldest, Keosha, thank you for being the "second mother" to your siblings and talking me through difficult situations. Courtney, as my middle child, your faith, relationship with God, and your constant pursuit of God caused me to do my best, to keep up with you. And to my namesake and only Son, George, Jr., you have been my quiet storm and one who was able to settle me down. I am so proud of what each of you have accomplished thus far in your lives and realize, that God is not finished with you. This book would not be possible without your support, encouragement, and belief in me. To my family, the Loves of my life, I dedicate this book to you.

Eternally Grateful!

FOREWORD

It is with great joy and humility that I write this foreword for my dear friend and fellow servant of the Lord, Pastor George Montgomery. For nearly two decades, I have had the privilege of knowing George both as a dedicated member of our congregation and as a faithful friend. Over these years, I have witnessed his unwavering commitment to his family, his faith, and his tireless pursuit of a deeper relationship and understanding of God's love.

In this book, "When I Was A Child: A Journey from Religion to Relationship," Pastor George Montgomery takes us on a remarkable and deeply personal journey. It is a journey that resonates with all who have grappled with the complexities of religion and the profound yearning for a genuine, transformative relationship with the Divine.

In the world of theology and ministry, it's not uncommon for individuals to get caught up in the trappings of religion—rituals, doctrines, and traditions—while losing sight of the heart of the gospel: the transformative power of a personal relationship with Jesus Christ. George's story is a testament to the fact that even those who stand in the pulpit are not immune to the struggles of faith.

Through the pages of this book, you will walk alongside Pastor George as he recounts his own journey, one that leads him from the confines of religious traditions to the boundless grace and love of a Savior who longs to know us intimately. With honesty and vulnerability, he shares the highs and lows, the doubts and certainties, and the profound encounters that shaped his path toward a richer, more authentic relationship with God.

Pastor George's story is not just his own—it is a story that speaks to the hearts of all seekers, to anyone who has ever questioned the status quo of faith, and to those who hunger for a more profound connection with the divine. His words will resonate with those who have felt trapped by religiosity and inspire those who long to discover the depths of God's unconditional love.

As a pastor, George Montgomery has dedicated his life to shepherding others toward a deeper walk with Christ, and this book is a continuation of that sacred calling. His willingness to share his journey so candidly is a testament to his desire to see others experience the transformative power of a relationship with God.

I encourage you to open the pages of "When I Was a Child" with an open heart and a willingness to engage with Pastor George's story. As you read, may you find encouragement, inspiration, and a renewed sense of hope in your spiritual journey. May you discover, as George did, that true faith is not found in rules and regulations, but in the beautiful, life-altering embrace of a Savior who loves you unconditionally.

It is my prayer that this book will serve as a beacon of light, guiding you toward a deeper, more authentic relationship with God, just as it has done for George and countless others. May you be blessed, challenged, and transformed by the profound truths found within these pages.

In Christ's love,

Senior Servant Cedric Johnson

Pastor of The Well Worship Center Ministries

INTRODUCTION

This book opens a window to a period of my life's journey which I have been blessed to experience. My journey started as a child, yes, I would say, even before my birth into this world. It has been a journey, much like many of you who has had to weather storms, endure failures, celebrate successes, learn from highs and lows, and to put it simply, navigate this thing we call life and somehow survive. If you are fortunate to have lived a life pleasing to the Father, I can say without a doubt, that you came through life with scars. But the scars were indicative that the Lord had purpose for you and in the end, the scars made you better and not bitter. I believe my story and experiences are like many of you who will read this book. Because of the similarities, some may say, then why did I write this book? If it is a retelling of what everyone has gone through, then everyone is familiar with how the story will go and how it ends. This is where the separation between what God has spoken to me and the path you have chosen to take.

This narrative was birthed in me from my earliest memories as a child. The passion to communicate my story has come and gone over the years as I became busy doing life. But no matter how much I procrastinated, no matter how much I turned away from speaking my truth, my truth as I experienced it, as I saw it and lived it, it lingered beneath the flesh and bones that my soul and spirit embodied. It was as if the fire had been put out, yet you could see the brightly lit embers beneath all my life's rubble and ash, still aflame. The prophet Jeremiah described his experience of fighting his destiny as it feeling like, "fire shut up in his bones." So, as I have started and stopped, and paused many times over the years while contemplating the writing of this book, I do so with the purpose that someone may read my story and realize it is not too late to change your destiny. This book is not intended or meant to cast shame or point fingers at any individuals, churches, fellowships, or denominations, although I am not naïve to the fact that there will be some who will take it as such, and in their spiritual realm, and attempt to "blacklist" and disassociate themselves from me, and what I have expressly stated as "my truth.' Somewhere between my truth and "the Truth," is where I hope you will discover God's divine purpose for why you're here, and what "HE" is calling you to.

I was birthed into The Church of God In Christ. I owe my foundation, upbringing, and understanding of what it means to live holy, to the Godly principles and beliefs of what was planted in me through COGIC. I will always maintain the standards that were embedded in me by many of the pioneers of this great church. But this book was not written to serve as a point of condemnation or referendum on COGIC, or any of the many movements, fellowships, ministries, or denominations that exist today. It is rather a warning to every individual, every ministry, every fellowship, and every denomination to guard itself against the embodied protocols and man-made traditions that have negatively impacted the spiritual relationship between the believer and the Lord Jesus Christ. We must endeavor to carry out the Great Commission, to Love the Lord with all of our heart, mind, and soul, and our neighbor as ourselves, and finally to prioritize our relationship with Christ above everything that clothes itself in the garments of Religion.

It is my sincere hope and earnest prayer that this book serves as a wake-up call to you as an individual and child of the Most High, and causes you to reflect on your journey and honestly assess and evaluate the question, "Is where you are today, a product of God's plan for your life or an overarching plan of manipulation and shrewd planning to get where you are." Because if you're not on the path and in the place the Lord desires you to be, then be careful, for you may gain the whole world, but lose your soul in the process.

CHAPTER 1

In The Beginning

As far back as I can remember my life seemed already planned out. I knew from early on that I was destined to be a preacher. Some of my earliest recollections involved my sister and I playing church in the living room of our apartment. I was about five or six years old at the time. No matter who led the testifying service or sang a song, I always ended up bringing the Word of God. My selection as the preacher was indeed a precursor of the calling I later acknowledged as a young boy. I recall catching the city bus to the Jerusalem Church of God In Christ where my family attended and my godfather, Dr. Albert Breckenridge, served as pastor. My godfather was a huge man in stature and whenever he spoke it was as if the heavens opened and gave way to thunderous sounds. He was my inspiration during those early years of my life and was in essence what a preacher should be.

My life was typical for a boy growing up in the projects of New Orleans, or so I thought. I went to school like my peers, did my homework and chores, and played football from sun up to sundown. This is where the comparisons shifted between me and my friends. While most of my friends and peers were running the streets, breaking curfew, and staying out half of the night, I could always be found sitting in church. If the church was opened, I was there. We were in church so much I can recall several times trying to hide in the neighborhood when it was church time. Seldom was this strategy successful as I, along with my mother, sisters, and brothers would find ourselves boarding the bus on our way to church. I would become quite angry and upset over having to stand at the bus stop with my church clothes on, as I watched my friends still playing games and having fun.

All my friends knew exactly where I was going because I was wearing my church clothes. One could always differentiate between church clothes, school clothes and play clothes. In my house, none of the children were ever allowed to play in our church or school clothes. Whenever my friends saw me at the bus stop, they didn't have to ask where I was going, all they had to do was observe what type of clothes I was wearing. When I was younger my mother would dress me up in little shorts, a dress shirt, and a tie. As I grew older, we did away with the shorts but I kept the dress shirt, and tie and eventually graduated to wearing a suit. Pretty soon I became known as the "church boy."

At the head of our family like most Black families, stood my grandmother, Viola Montgomery. "Grandma," as we affectionately called her was the matriarch of our family. She instilled the spiritual, moral, and ethical foundation within my mother, four sisters, and two older brothers. Grandma was the centerpiece of what kept us united and strong as a family unit. She had a marvelous sense of humor, strict to the core, and yet so much fun to be around. Although she never received any formal education and as a youth could not read her own name if she saw it in "boxcar letters," she was a woman of tremendous wisdom, insight, and intelligence. She was proud to tell anyone who asked that she learned how to read by reading the bible. The thing that stood out about Grandma was that she was a woman who believed in God and was not ashamed to let everybody she encountered know it. Grandma was a living history lesson, being born in 1893 and living for more than a century. It was fascinating sitting down at her feet and hearing her tell countless tales of past civic, religious, and cultural events that occurred during her lifetime.

A licensed missionary in the Church of God In Christ, Grandma often told us how she evangelized and "worked out" fourteen separate churches across Louisiana and East Texas and turned them over to male preachers to pastor. During her day and still, within our denomination, women could minister the word of God as missionaries or evangelists but are not ordained to hold the office or title of pastor or preacher. Still today if you hear the word woman and pastor in the same sentence it is almost tantamount to blasphemy. Grandma had a favorite saying, **"I may not be a preacher or a preacher's son, but I can hold a church together until a preacher comes."** This was the motto she lived by and her zeal for Christ was evident by the way she praised God, lived her life, and taught the Word of God. Even though our denomination did not ordain women as elders or appoint them as pastors there were not many preachers who could "out preach" my grandmother. When she would go forth in the Word, she would lift her voice up and literally sing her message, (or what we called "tune-up"). **"Tuning up" in the Pentecostal church is where you put a little gravy to the meat of your message and proclaim the gospel in voice tones that rise and fall, ebb, and flow in a melodic symphony** (or what we commonly refer to as "hooping"). When she would have finished preaching the saints would be praising God, shouting halleluiah, and "laid out" in the spirit. Whenever Grandma, or Mother Montgomery as she was affectionately known across church circles prayed, sang, shouted, or ministered the Word of God, saints, and sinners would gather from all around to see this dynamo in action. Although she only stood about 5'2 inches tall and seemed to weigh less than one hundred pounds, it was apparent that God condensed a "giant" anointing and placed it inside of her tiny frame.

Growing up I heard countless testimonies from people stating as they approached the sanctuary from blocks away, they could hear Mother Montgomery's voice above the music and singing that was taking place inside the church. She tells the story that while sitting under a tree in Lake Charles, Louisiana, a preacher was passing by and laid his hands upon her head and decreed a special anointing rest upon her life. She would come to discover that the person who laid his hands on her was none other than the late Bishop Charles Harrison Mason, the founding father of the Church of God In Christ. Grandma carried her enthusiasm for serving the Lord into every part of her life. As a strict disciplinarian, there was not much a person could get away with around her. It was as if she had a direct pipeline into your kitchen, bedroom, or wherever you thought you could do wrong and hide. Even though she was limited in her formal education, I now know that she was operating in the divine gifts of Discernment, Word of Knowledge, and Word of Wisdom. Grandma was a stickler for holy living. She always told me, **"If you're gonna be a saint, then be one 100% all the way. But if you're gonna be a devil, then be one 100% and go to hell having a ball."** She would tell us that before she got saved, she would dance all night for the devil. And now that she was saved, she felt like God deserved better. Everything she did she did with all her might. She became the earthen vessel God used to light a fire inside of me causing me to desire to come to know the Jesus she served. Not only was she my entrance to a relationship with the Lord but she ultimately became the cornerstone of faith for my children and so many who would connect spiritually with the Montgomery family over the years.

My spiritual genesis exposed me to church services where the laying on of hands went forth, people would speak in other tongues and some would go forth in a holy dance, or what we called "shouting." You knew you had church when people would fall out under the power of the Holy Ghost or after the benediction had been given and the saints had to be helped to their car still speaking in tongues. There were times when church would end and it would be another hour or two before people were able to leave the building as a result of the powerful outpouring of God's presence upon the people. At my home church where I received the baptism of the Holy Ghost, the Spirit would be so powerful that at times when you looked up at the top of the ceiling you would see smoke literally filled the church. The building itself was very small and could seat between 50 and 60 people but when the glory of the Lord showed up, it was as if everyone had lit up a cigarette and continuously puffed smoke in the air. **In my mind, this is what I imagined what it must have looked like inside the Holy of Holies whenever the presence of God would show up.** This is the image I imagined Isaiah saw when he described the Lord's train filling the temple in Isaiah Chapter 6.

This would be part of my beginning and the backdrop to the public calling on my life. It was here that God began to manifest me to the world even though I had no understanding of such things at the time. Reflecting on my beginning now I realize that being reared in the projects of New Orleans, growing up in a single-parent home, being a child born out of wedlock, and having to go through and endure the experiences and challenges of my youth, was God's way of preparing and conditioning me for what was to come. **The early years of my childhood and those leading up to adolescence became the crucible that forged my character and jump-started me on a collision course with God.**

CHAPTER 2

When I Was A Child

I was unaware of it at the time but as I grew older, I came to learn my childhood became the foundational platform for what became my indoctrination into the phenomenon known as "The church." Before you jump to predetermined judgments about this book, let me clearly state there is nothing wrong with "the church." Without the presence and influence of the church, most of us would be in a terrible mess. It was through the ministry of a church member or church-related event that captured our hearts and led us to salvation. I remain concerned of what we mistakenly identify as "the church" today has become the predominant factor in our relationship with God rather than cultivating a "true relationship" with the Father. The real crisis is when church, not relationship, becomes so ingrained in our spiritual walk that it seizes priority status as the center of our life.

The apostle Paul wrote in 1 Corinthians 13:11, **"When I was a child, I spake as a child, I understood as a child, I thought as a child: but when became a man, I put away childish things."** When I think of a child's nature, they are most vulnerable in their formative years. Their personality, mannerisms, perspectives on life, and overall development are inextricably tied to the influences of those surrounding them on a frequent and consistent basis. Like a normal child's brain development, pliability is greatest at the earliest levels in the maturation process. It was in my early and formative years that I became akin to a piece of canvas, displayed, and positioned for men to paint their opinions, ideas, and philosophies onto. In error, I yielded the innocence of my youth to the "Fathers and Mothers" of the church. Many of these individuals were more concerned about teaching people "their way" instead of God's way. I became a willing co-conspirator of my demise and got entangled in the practice of making gods out of mortal men. Instead of growing up like a lump of clay waiting to be molded by the master craftsman, I became a paint-by-the-numbers stencil in the hands of men. Knowing God for myself became more challenging for me as I found myself knowing God through the eyes of others. The "Old Boys Club" was hard at work right before my eyes and I did not even discern it. I had come to observe by word and deed that the way to go up in the church was to fall in line and "praise" the current church leadership. Those who held the power and positions would notice that and when ecclesiastical opportunities became available, those would be the ones considered for promotion. The message that was communicated to anyone desiring to be in leadership was that promotion came from the leader, whether it was on the local, district, state, or national level, and not necessarily the Lord.

It was not until many years later after becoming a parent myself, I realized the awesome responsibility we have on imparting life into the spirit of our sons and daughters. I came to understand that if you are not intentional regarding the things of the Lord, you can easily find yourself "shaping" and "projecting" your agendas and issues onto those coming behind you. If you are not careful it is so easy and self-appeasing to slip into the mold of creating little replicas of yourself. Most of us see ourselves in a much different light than who we are and how others see us. For some, it is difficult to face our true selves and as a result, we end up living a life that reflects our "make-believe" selves. We spend a lot of time convincing ourselves that we are the best person we can be, and either never try or stop trying to discover the deeper part of ourselves out of fear of who we may discover under the façade of what we have portrayed for so many years. We are quicker to believe the LIE about who we are NOT than the Truth about who we are! For most of us, all the self-help books, seminars, and personal development workshops only help to perpetuate the image that we desire others to see but not the one God longs for us to expose. We spend a lifetime raising children and leaders not in the "way they should go" but rather in the way that we want them to go.

Parenting can be a traumatic life experience in and of itself. It will cause a parent to ask, "Have I followed God's divine will in raising my child, or have I groomed my child to be **what I wanted** them to be?" As parents and leaders, we often spend more time *"showing"* the way than *"being"* the way. Jesus understood the difference when he declared to his disciples, "I am the way."

It is natural for the creation to resemble its creator. Most parents look at their children and project what might have been for themselves (IF ONLY)! I believe parents genuinely desire the best for their offspring. Where the mistake comes in is when we lose ourselves in our children and attempt to "relive" our lives through our sons and daughters. We somehow convince ourselves that if we could redo our own "extreme makeover" we would eliminate past failures and the result would be this new, improved, and mistake-free version of ourselves. We fail to grasp the reality of how easy it is to rubber-stamp our personalities, dreams, and fears on our children. We forget how impressionable and vulnerable young children are. Let us pause for a moment and investigate the nature and characteristics that are readily found in the life of a child.

Part of a child's nature and character is to be trusting, easily influenced, easily led, and quick to believe what he or she is told. A child will usually comply with the requests of adults, especially if trust has been earned. Children crave acceptance and approval. The child usually assumes that those older than himself have his best interests at heart. Adults are supposed to protect their children. Adults are supposed to work for what is in the best interest of the child. In the field of Child Welfare, those are some of the basic norms and expectations every child has the right to receive. That is why we are not shocked when we hear of incidents where children willingly get into cars with strangers. It is not the first instinct of a child to be defiant or oppositional. We are usually taken aback by a child who questions authority or refuses to comply with what they have been asked by adults. A child exemplifying this sort of behavior is usually labeled by society as "defiant" or "oppositional." Child-like characteristics I described earlier are normally associated with sheep and lambs biblically. Christ identifies himself as "the Good Shepherd" in St. John 10:11 and refers to us as sheep and lambs. The sheep are dependent on the shepherd for food, guidance, shelter, and protection. Without the shepherd, sheep will become lost, disoriented, malnourished, and ultimately destroyed by their natural enemies. I followed the teaching of the church and took on the spirit of the lamb. I became such a lamb, that I felt like I needed someone else, a visionary, to see for me. I humbled myself as a child before his spiritual fathers, choosing to surrender control of my destiny to others. Rather than earnestly seeking God for what his will for me was, I acquiesced to becoming a pawn in the gamesmanship of "churchdom," and spiritual leaders. I cannot recall the number of times I heard Ephesians 6:1, "Children, obey your parents in the Lord: for this is right," preached in my hearing and the hearing of other congregants. I became dependent on others to see, develop, and unleash the potential that was locked inside this boy from the projects. It was as if the leadership of the church had convened one of its conferences and said, "So here is another one that we can train, another one that will ultimately do our bidding. Let us make another church member. Let us make him into our image and after our likeness." And when they had completed the process, they "saw that it was good." Do these words sound familiar? Unfortunately, this was not the convening of the Divine Triune Godhead amid creation, rather this was the earthly mindset of the "spirit of religion" at its best.

My entire upbringing, although not emanating from having any preachers, pastors, or bishops in my family seemed to be geared toward being "rubber-stamped" in the factory of religion. At six years old I heard the call to ministry but because I did not fully understand what that meant, I did not acknowledge my call to ministry until the age of eleven. Although I stood with no clue as to what ministry was all about, I was eager and willing to sit at the feet of those more capable than I and learn. What I did not recognize at the time was God had placed in me the heart of a servant. Servanthood I learned was what true ministry is all about. I was always willing and made myself available when opportunities to learn from godly men and women came along. I was destined to equip myself to do just that – **SERVE**. Jesus said of himself in Matthew 20:28, "The Son of man came not to be ministered unto, but to minister." I began my apprenticeship by serving the church in a variety of ways. When other children were busy playing games with each other, I could be found sitting in adult bible classes soaking up knowledge and wisdom that is often found in mature saints. I know that my love for wanting to be around older adults stemmed from my relationship with my grandmother. Although my mother was in the house, I was influenced primarily by my grandmother. I remember jumping out of my bedroom window and running away to her house to escape a pending consequence from one of my older sisters. I was eleven at the time I ran away to my grandmother's and resided with her until I went off to college. I was always an "old soul trapped inside a young man's body." I developed a thirst and passion for wanting to know more and more about the bible. Now and then I would take a chance at answering one of the difficult questions in the adult bible classes, as we had no children's ministry classes at the time. And to everyone's surprise, now and then I would come up with the correct answer. This created inside of me an insatiable passion to learn how to "rightfully divide the word of truth."

CHAPTER 3

A Good Soldier

I began a lengthy and meticulous process of being indoctrinated by the spirit of religion. I bought into the concept of church, "hook, line, and sinker," as the vehicle that would usher me into the next phase of my life. Without being fully aware, I surrendered my purpose for the greater cause of the Ecclesiastical Hierarchy of my denomination. In my zeal to fall in line with the program, I opened my spirit to being spoken over but not spoken into. I was trained on how to carry out various church tasks but not mentored on allowing the gifts of the Lord to flow for his glory. I had become a project that was being molded and shaped for church work. What I did not grasp at the time was a person could do church work and still not be involved in true ministry. One could master the work of church over time and still not be acquainted with the "Master" of the work. I was well acquainted with Sunday School, Young Peoples Willing Workers, better known as YPWW, and the Music and Evangelism ministries as I had served as a leader in many of these departments. Still, the true essence of what ministry was all about was somehow obscured from me. In my earlier years, the term *minister* was always used to differentiate the preacher's role as being separate from the rest of the Body of Christ. It was during my teen years when I came to the revelation that every believer, not just the preacher, is called to minister to others. I had been exposed to the philosophy and environment predicated upon the assertion that only preachers were ministers, everyone else was just members who served. And whenever serving was involved it was always leadership being served by the members, and never vice-versa. The only time I observed pastors serving was during the times when feet washing was a part of the communion service and pastors would wash the feet of their congregants. Whenever I heard the term minister or ministry, I inevitably thought it referred to the preacher and not the people. I had come to believe ministry was getting up before a congregation and preaching the Word of God. The Lord later revealed to me in Romans 12: 4-8, that although members of the church were "ONE BODY," we are all called to ministry through our varying spiritual gifts.

In our church, we sang a song entitled, "I'm a Soldier in the Army of the Lord." It was the soldier's mentality that I soon found myself emerging in with no knowledge or awareness that I had become one of them, a "good soldier." A good soldier is not inclusive of any denomination, any reformation, any church, any movement, or any group of believers. There is nothing wrong with being a soldier in the Lord's army. But inherent in becoming a soldier in any army is you are trained to obey orders. **The dilemma occurs when it becomes difficult to discern a "good" soldier from a "God" soldier.** The problem exists when you are confronted with the challenge of deciding whose orders you will ultimately obey – Man's or God's. It is not as easy to do as it may sound especially when false teaching and erroneous interpretation of scripture are presented to you as "the Lord speaking." This coupled with a young Christian's desire to please their leader makes the challenge of discernment even more difficult. The Apostles came under this same scrutiny when threatened with further persecution at the hands of the high priest and Sadducees if they failed to agree to cease preaching anymore in Jesus' name. They responded in Acts 5:29 by declaring, "We ought to obey God rather than men."

I was born into the Church of God In Christ as a third-generation member. From my earliest memories of the denomination, I was indebted to the organization for its standard of holiness, its teachings, and its emphasis on holy living. Without the COGIC I would not be where I am today. It was the COGIC's teaching that molded me and became the foundation on which my character was developed. I want to be extremely clear my intent is not to discredit or indict the Church of God In Christ or its importance to the Body of Christ in any way. "A good soldier" is not confined to any particular denomination. You will find good soldiers in the Methodist Church, Full Gospel Baptist, Apostolic, Pentecostal, Assembly of God, Missionary Baptist, AME Zion, Lutheran, Presbyterian, Catholic, or any other church group or denominational body. "A good soldier" usually refers to one who refuses to rock the boat, the one who goes along with the program, the one whom everyone speaks well of, and the one who is on the path to greatness as defined by the denomination's leadership. Yes, that one! The one who is next in line, the one who is being groomed to take over, the one labeled as the next golden boy or girl, and the one who follows orders without dissent. Yes, that one! All of us have been or at least have seen good soldiers in every setting, whether it is on the job, in school, or in the church.

CHAPTER 4

The Glory Of The First House

Several years ago, I attended a church convention that was held in Baltimore,

Maryland. Although I was only there for a limited time, what I observed firsthand literally broke my heart. The convention had always been a source of inspiration, especially for the youth of my denomination. It was a place where the saints came to fellowship, learn more about the Lord, enhance our spiritual walk, develop positive and lasting friendships, and receive information that they could take back to their local assemblies and implement on a grassroots level. This convention had always been on the "cutting edge" of ministry, a place where both young and mature were provided essential training for the expansion of the "work." This convention proved to be especially instrumental in promoting the youth of the church from the crawling to walking stages. Here you were exposed to some of the most prolific speakers, presenters, and craftsmen Christendom has ever seen. Various departments of the denomination, Sunday School, Evangelism, Mission, Youth, and Music came together for an entire week of training and celebration. Youth from across the nation, and even other parts of the world, gathered to learn from the "Masters." This is where the future preachers, evangelists, missionaries, visionaries, and servants of the church shined their brightest.

It was this type of experience that I expected to see when I arrived in Baltimore. What I saw instead was something that I was not prepared for. The first encounter I had with the convention was on Friday morning. Here, I was blessed to hear one of the truly remarkable pastors of our time, Brandon Porter of Memphis, Tennessee. He was serving then in the capacity of the President of the Youth Department for our denomination. He preached a message that touched on relationships and knowing you. It truly was an inspired word from the Lord. At a time when the church appeared to be ignoring the youth and trying to impose its will on them, he appeared to be one of the lone and strongest voices advocating for youth to be able to express themselves for who they were.

Midway through his message something caught my attention that ultimately would leave me at a loss for words. As I visually panned the audience, I began to notice that in an audience of approximately four thousand people, it appeared the only ones paying attention were the three hundred persons gathered around the pulpit area (none of which appeared to be under twenty-five years of age). I know there were many more persons who were listening, but it just seemed like every person under twenty-five, was more concerned with other things. There for the entire world to see were thousands of people talking on their cell phones, holding conversations, renewing acquaintances, or making other plans on the floor of the convention center. It was evident that talking to someone else had become more of a priority than hearing what God had to say through his spoken word. I suddenly realized that the convention that I once knew as a "glory cloud" had morphed into nothing more than an enormous social gathering.

That evening, Bishop G.E. Patterson, the late presiding prelate of the Church of God In Christ, was the featured speaker and the main hall of the convention center was packed. When I arrived at the center at approximately 6:00 p.m., the room was about three-quarters full. Not long afterward, the room quickly filled up, numbering what appeared to be approximately 10 to 15 thousand people. This night was a night of pomp and circumstance as the Chief Apostle of the denomination was the featured speaker. Children were on display waving banners and dancing, youth step teams performed, and the choir lifted jubilant praises in song. The giving of the seed was orchestrated in such a unique and jubilant manner that saints were dancing in the aisles. The environment was filled with an air of "expectancy" as the people of God anticipated a Word from the Lord. The stage was set for a mighty visitation of the Holy Spirit. But just as I had done earlier in the day's session, I began to survey the audience and witnessed so many persons, young and old alike casually walking and talking inside the ballroom where Bishop was scheduled to speak. Many could be seen talking on their cell phones while others paraded around the great hall as if in a fashion show. It was as if no one came to "get in the presence of God." Many came to see each other, but not God; many came to showcase their talents but not to worship; many came to be seen but not to seek; many came to have church but not to hear from God. It appeared most were only concerned with getting phone numbers, exchanging the latest gossip, finding out where the best eating and shopping places were, and just hanging out and looking good and important. As I watched this display of church conduct, my spirit became overwhelmed with grief, and I started to openly weep. Now before you go judging me and thinking that I believed everyone in the room was wrong and I was the only one right, let me take you back to an experience I had many years ago.

When I was about 15 years old, I remember foolishly thinking that I was the only young child saved. I would go to various church services and it always seemed like I was the only young person inside the church that was saved and trying to live right (of course this was my own exaggerated and deluded sense of what I perceived). It seemed as if everyone else was outside socializing or trying to exchange phone numbers to set up dates. But it was not until I went to the Holy Convocation in Memphis, Tennessee, that I saw young people on "fire" for the Lord. God allowed me to see other young people who were just as, if not more, zealous as I was. They were going forth in ministry, speaking, preaching, reciting poetic pieces, singing, shouting, and witnessing in ways that I had only dreamed about. Those young people, and others like them, filled my heart with pride and humility at the same time. I was proud to be a part of a church that had so many "gifts" operating in the body of Christ. I knew that the denomination I grew up in, was "right" because holiness was taught as the standard for living. I was also humbled by the experience, because it taught me that, like the prophet Elijah in 1 Kings 19:18, God had thousands more who had not "bowed to Baal." This was one of the "wake-up" calls I received at an early age that allowed me to see my potential in the body of Christ.

But as I looked at what the church, and especially the youth had evolved into, I was deeply saddened. For I understood all too well what was once important to us (the church's youth), had ceased to be important any longer. What was the hallmark of our identity? A holy lifestyle was replaced by the modernism of technology and fashions of the day. The Louis Vuitton purse hanging from our shoulder had replaced the King James Bible in our hand. We were now more concerned about wearing the gold and silver crosses that hung around our necks than wearing the mantle of the Holy Spirit. We were now more interested in getting in touch with our friends, via cell phone and internet than getting in touch with the Lord, via prayer.

I felt like standing up amid that great aggregation of people and screaming to the top of my voice, to get everyone's attention to tell them that they had left their first love. For when I looked around for worship, I saw indifference; when I looked for praise, I saw entertainment; when I sought God's presence, I saw people more concerned with getting a "hook-up." This was not the place where I "found" myself as a young child. This was not the place where the torch of God's fire, had once been ignited in my heart. Gatherings like this are where I came to understand God had thousands upon thousands who were also saved. It was in venues like this that I started to grow up to understand what God's purpose was for me. Like Joseph of old, God granted me a preview of my future, while I was still residing in my present.

But "this place" had now become the place of disillusionment; it was now the place of unfulfillment and unfulfilled dreams; it was the place where, like Daniel 5:27, we were "weighed in the balances and found wanting." This place had become an empty place; void of the anointing of God and his power; it had ceased to be the place of miracles and had become the place where the residue of miracles lingered. It was like having an object sitting in a place for some time and when moved from its spot, all that is left visible is the impression of where it had previously been positioned. From time to time I get in the mood to change around a couch or bed in my house. Every time I move a piece of furniture, I can always identify the exact place where it used to rest. Why, because it always leaves an impression on the carpet flooring. As I surveyed this vast audience, I could sense in the spirit that "this place" was the place of God's residue. It is where God had been, but no longer was. The saddest thing for me to come to grips with was realizing people were oblivious to the fact that they were dwelling in the "residue" of God's presence, and not his fullness. Witnessing a similar condition of the church long ago, the prophet Haggai said in Chapter 2:3, "**Who is left among you that saw this house in her first glory? And how do you see it now? Is it not in your eyes in comparison to it as nothing?**" Although I did not see the Church of God In Christ in her first glory, which was the time of Bishop Mason, I did see this church in the early '60s and '70s when Bishop J.O. Patterson, Sr. was taking this denomination from the backwoods of society to the forefront of Christendom. And like the children of Israel were commanded to tell what their eyes had seen, and their ears had heard concerning their deliverance from the hand of Pharaoh and the land of Egypt, my grandmother, and saints of old, would testify about the church's glory days. She would talk about seeing blinding eyes opened, deaf ears unstopped, the lame walking, people coming into the church drunk and leaving saved and sober, and the visible presence of the Lord in the building. "This House" that I now was observing, had lost its first glory and was unrecognizable to me. It was not the house of my grandmother or even my youth anymore. What was once a body of believers who touted the principles of holy living and sanctification had become, like the children of Israel and the golden calf, a group of "idol worshippers." This was the place where Pentecostals looked for guidance and direction. COGIC was set apart, above the rest, and knew it; but now, if you threw them in a group along with other denominations, you would be hard-pressed to identify who was COGIC and who was Non-Denominational, Baptist, or Charismatic. I was taught as a child that according to St. Matthew 5:14, "We are the light of the world, a city that is set on a hill cannot be hidden." Unfortunately, I was also taught in error, that that light was the exclusive property of the Church of God In Christ. What I discovered after I began to grow and mature was that God's light was not exclusive to any denomination or church, but rather, the sole property of every believer in the Body of Christ.

Who is left that saw this house in her first glory? The answer is a simple one…not many! I believe that is one of the reasons for the discrepancy in what we now identify as holiness, which is markedly different than the "standard" that our forefathers established many years ago. The people of today have no real standard by which to measure up against. What they have taken for holiness, is watered-down and compromised living. Miracles have been replaced by "feel-good" shouting and dancing. True prophetic utterances have been replaced by "get ready to be blessed proclamations." I recall growing up and even in my teen years, trying to position myself in just the right spot, sitting behind a sister's big hat, hoping the prophet would not see me and call me out and expose the sinful thing I had done that day or week. But nowadays, people flock to go and see the prophet. Instead of trying to hide from the man or woman of God, folks dress up extravagantly to be noticed, or "show out" in such a fashion during service, hoping to be singled out to receive a prophetic word about a new home, money in the mail, or some unexpected blessing that is coming their way. I cannot recall the last time I saw a prophet call out someone and pronounce a warning to someone about sanctifying themselves. Today prophetic conferences have become gloried Christmas giveaways and people by the thousands will travel hundreds of miles in hopes of receiving a "word" from the man or woman of God. Sadly, and regrettably, this house has become "as nothing."

CHAPTER 5

THE ESSENCE OF TRADITION

As I grew older and matured, I became exposed to many teachings and traditions of the church. My face-to-face encounter with man's traditions led me to call them ***"the good, the bad, and the ugly."*** The *"good"* is centered on being taught biblical principles of holy living. Contrary to what some churches might believe, "holiness or holy living," is not the domain of any particular religious denomination or ministry. Not only is holiness available to every believer, but every believer is called to live a life of holiness as clearly stated in Hebrews 12:14, "holiness, without which no man shall see the Lord". The denomination that I grew up in was fundamental in its teaching and emphasized moral, ethical, and spiritual purity here on earth. So, I grew up thinking that one could live a perfect life while here on earth just as Jesus stated in St. Matthew 5:48, "Be ye therefore perfect, even as your Father which is in heaven is perfect." I believed this perfection meant that once saved, you could live on earth without committing a single sin. So, I strived to live the perfect life, which meant no lying, backbiting, cheating, as well as all other forms of sin. Now I know you think I am crazy because people believe that no one can live "free from sin," once they have given their life to Jesus. But we were taught otherwise. Let me give you an example: say you were a liar, a thief, a fornicator, and a gossiper. After conquering the urge to fornicate and steal, you became perfect and eliminated your flaws in these two specific areas. Now, you still had to work on getting the areas of gossiping and lying under subjection, but in the areas of thievery and fornication, you would have conquered and perfected yourself in these two areas. Although you have not reached perfection at this point, you are in the process of moving toward the "mark of the prize of the high calling which is in Christ Jesus." The apostle Paul goes on to admonish the body of Christ in Philippians 3:15, "let us therefore, as many as be perfect, be thus minded."

This teaching sounded good and was appealing to the natural ear. But let us examine this doctrine a little closer. First, this scripture was not talking about earthly perfection in the sense that a person will not ever make a mistake. Roman 3:23 teaches us "that all have sinned and come short of the glory of God," and the fact that we have an advocate and intercessor, in the person of Jesus Christ, indicates man's predisposition to sin. The act of becoming perfect had reference to a spiritual maturation process that every believer will experience if they are to fulfill the destiny ordained by our heavenly father. 1 Corinthians 13:11 gives the narrative, "When I was a child, I spake as a child, I understood as a child, I thought as a child: but when I became a man, I put away childish things." In addition, the apostle Paul tells us to "desire the sincere milk of the word that we may grow thereby." This growth process represents the Christian's maturation in Christ. If our children failed to grow physically, mentally, or emotionally year after year, we would quickly take them to see a doctor, recognizing that something was stunting their growth process. As it is in the natural, so it is in the spirit. If a believer walks with God year after year and fails to mature spiritually, then something inevitably is wrong. So, the tradition of one being able to live a godly life and a lifestyle of holiness while present in this world, became a solid foundation for me as I continued to mature in Christ.

However, as I grew a little older and wiser, mixed in with the good were some striking resemblances to the "ways of the Pharisee." I was taught in depth about the "letter and traditions" of the church but had superficial instruction when it came to learning about "intimacy with the Spirit." This was the *"bad"* that I had found at the heart of religious tradition. Traditions in and of themselves are not terrible things. Many people look at traditions with scorn and renounce their very existence. I know that many traditions are honorable, and we should seek to keep and promulgate some of them among the people of God. Every great civilization and successful institution that has ever existed has had its share of honored and lasting traditions. It is only when we allow the "spirit of tradition" to govern and dictate our destiny and God's purpose for our lives that we find ourselves in trouble. Tradition is partly to blame for blinding the eyes of the religious leaders of Jesus' day from recognizing Jesus as the Messiah. Instead of seeing Jesus as the King of Kings, tradition dictated that he was merely the son of a carpenter. Tradition said it was not lawful to heal on the Sabbath. Tradition said a righteous man would not keep company with harlots and publicans. Tradition said royalty was birthed in a palace and not a stable. Tradition said if you were a man of God, then your place was in the synagogue – and not the open marketplace. And finally, tradition said that if you were a king, you would not die among common thieves and be buried in a borrowed tomb. Tradition looks at "what should be" and fails to recognize the exception. The tradition lives and survives on "what is to be expected" while negating and remaining blind to "the unexpected." Tradition seeks out and is most comfortable resting in the past, while the Spirit embraces and points to the future. Someone once said that the definition of insanity is, "doing the same thing over and over and expecting different results." That is a little bit of what tradition does. It keeps you going in the same direction and with the same methodologies that ultimately produce more of the same results. But when I looked at the life of Jesus and the great men and women of God whose life stories are revealed in the Word of God, I cannot help but see men and women who went against the tradition; people who defied the usual produced the unexpected and set out in new and challenging directions. It was people like Paul who preached the gospel to the Gentiles, Abraham who left his place of familiarity for a land that he did not know of, or Noah who dared to build a vessel that would float on water, even though to that point it had never rained on the earth before. Talk about bucking tradition? How about a deliverer who had a death sentence on him, or a king who laid the foundation of what it means to worship the Lord in song; or how about a prostitute who taught later generations the true meaning of worship? This is what tradition prohibits. It dares anyone or anything to be different. A noted bishop's wife once said to their congregation, "We're the way we are because we are the way we are, and don't come here trying to change that." What an indictment for change and a call for the status quo from one who operates in authority in the church. That statement was directly aimed at my wife and my attempt to bring a different perspective and new outlook of ministry to that local church. That church had become locked in the bowels of tradition and had fortified itself against all "outsiders." An outsider was anyone who did not think, look, or act like they did. One of the favorite scriptures of the pastor of the church was Jeremiah 6:16 which says, "Thus saith the Lord, stand ye in the ways, and see, and ask for the old paths, where is the good way, and walk therein, and ye shall find rest for your souls." The pastor would use this verse of scripture to combat anyone or anything that appeared to be contemporary or different from what they had become accustomed to. If you were thought to be innovative or creative in your approach to the church or its programs, then you would be quickly labeled a radical or someone operating with "this modern-day Holy Ghost." You were quickly singled out and treated as if you had contracted some contagious disease. Everything modern or contemporary was inherently bad for some strange reason. Yet when I looked at the mode of transportation of the pastor, his wife, and family, it was always the latest model cars – and not old jalopies. They dressed impeccably, with the latest fashions – and you were hard-pressed to see them in the same outfit more than two or three times within the same year. In a day when the world is "bling blinging," they wore the best of jewelry – from diamonds to sapphires. And of course, their home was equipped with the most modern and up-to-date technological devices and gadgets. Now am I suggesting God's people do not deserve to look good, drive good, eat good, or live good? NEVER!

Today this seems like an absurd assumption, although at one time I must confess that I had the impression that the "poorer you were, the more saved you were, and the more God could use you. I mean, after all, Jesus himself told a rich man, that it was as "hard for a rich man to enter into the kingdom of heaven as it was for a camel to go through the eye of a needle." And of course, when I would hear this scripture taught, it was interpreted in a very literal sense. Imagine me reconciling a person of wealth trying to get into the kingdom in the same way a camel would attempt to squeeze through the eye of a literal sewing needle. It never was taught that the body of Christ could be more effective in the kingdom and have a far greater witnessing impact if we all looked good, lived well, and were prosperous. Many pastors taught that the leader was God's chosen vessel and as your representative to the world, had a mandate by God to go "first class." It did not matter if the congregation had the financial resources to provide for themselves, as long as they took care of the leader. If that meant, having your lights cut off, so be it. If that meant not having adequate food in your house to feed your children, oh well. If that meant you sending your Pastor and wife on vacation while you stayed at home, God bless you. It had even become common practice for certain leaders to admonish the members to go to their favorite banking institution and secure a loan to ensure their leaders were blessed financially. In our denomination, each member and leader of the local church was assessed a financial amount which was to be paid at set times throughout the year for various conventions and church meetings. There were more times than I care to remember when I would somehow manage to scrape together my report or assessment to send the pastor, bishop, superintendent, or district missionary to a convention, only to find myself stuck at home because I did not have enough funds left, to send myself. As an adult, I began to think how wonderful it would be if the local, district, and jurisdictional fellowships would step up and select individuals and married couples who had never been to certain state and national meetings and pay for their travel and housing expenses. This would send a message to the laity, especially those who have never experienced national meetings, such as the Holy Convocation, that the church does care and is concerned about you. I would often hear pastors, or those advocating for his financial benefit quote the scripture in 1 Timothy 5:18, "Thou shalt not muzzle the ox that treadeth out the corn" or " the laborer is worthy of his hire." Being a former senior pastor myself, I certainly agree with this verse of scripture and support every pastor's hope of being supported financially by his congregants. But I wonder why this same scripture is never quoted when it comes to the president or leader of a local church auxiliary; or could an usher or church greeter be viewed as a laborer? What about the person who cleans the church, drives the church van, maintains the grounds, or works with the music and art department…are they treading out any corn, and if so, do they qualify in not being muzzled as well? How many people would not visit or join the local church if the grounds were maintained in a deplorable condition? How many returning visitors would the local assembly have if they did not experience the warm and friendly embrace of a greeter or usher, who served them with excellence? How many would come to the church musical if the choir sounded awful? So, when we apply scripture to honor the leader, we must always be cognizant that effective and impactful leaders come in every capacity and some, you would not even think of.

The *"ugly"* I would have to say, was coming to grips with the true personalities of church leaders. As a boy growing up in the church, you must understand that I was surrounded by people whom I had looked up to and admired virtually all of my life. For as long as I can remember, these people, Pastors and Missionaries, Bishops and State Supervisors, Evangelists, and Mothers have been my modern-day heroes and heroines. These were the people whom I had spent years listening to, being taught by, being exposed to, and being trained by. I was beginning to be elevated to certain positions within the district and jurisdictional levels of the church. These new leadership positions afforded me opportunities to interact with some of the people I had admired over the years. What had formerly been teacher-pupil relationships, had become co-worker and peer relationships because of ecclesiastical promotions that I was now occupying. Although I was still in awe of the personalities of "who these people were," I was now called upon to work side by side, and in some cases, to lead some of the very people I had admired for so many years. Talk about a "mindset" change. This introduction, this baptism by fire behind the façade of what had appeared to be one thing, had now become ugly. I had now come face to face with who people were behind the masks of appearances. And I hated it. I fought so hard to stay in a state of "innocence" when interacting with certain members of our denomination's leadership. These people were saved, upright, and men and women of great standing in the church. The Lord had to deal with me by removing the blinders off my eyes to see people for who they were, and not who they pretended to be. This called for a reality check on my part.

I can recall on one occasion while working as the Jurisdictional Youth Department Chairman, coming up with an innovative idea to incorporate a program designed for the youth of the jurisdiction. I was asked to seek out, share my ideas, and work cooperatively with the representative of another Jurisdictional department in implementing a program that the Lord had given me.

Well to my surprise my counterpart rebuffed my efforts, refused to work with me, gave me a very cold shoulder, and generally ignored my ideas. And if you think that was a surprise, imagine my feelings when this same person who did not give me the time of day unveiled and presented my original idea as their own. Welcome to "Church Backstabbing 101." I was devastated by the deceptive and manipulative tactics of someone whom I thought the world of. I questioned God about this situation and told him I did not want to see this and asked, why was he showing me "that" side of people. The Lord responded by telling me I needed to discern people for who they were. He went on to let me know that where he was taking me, I needed "open" eyes. I needed to see the ugly and flawed side of persons who had been representing themselves as Christians, but in fact either had no real relationship with him at all, had walked away from him and were now operating in the flesh, or at best, had a very superficial relationship with him. This was a time I had to grow up, and even though it meant exposing people whom I had long admired, God told me it was needful for me to see past the masquerade people presented. As I look back now, this was the point where I lost my innocence and naiveté to the church world around me. In a way, it was as if I had lost my "spiritual virginity" to the old vanguard of the church. I felt violated. The feeling was similar to the time when my home was broken into, and things were stolen from me. I have heard rape victims talk about feeling sexually violated, and although I do not report to know what that feels like, I think there are some similarities between the two. At a time when I wanted to stay "closed-eyed" and in awe of certain personalities, the Lord said, LOOK! And in looking, I got an eye-opening look into the spirit of the leaders of our denomination. It remains to this day, a sight that I did not welcome or cherish to see. But it was the ugly that helped usher me to the next level in God. The Lord let me know that with every level of promotion, both in the Spirit and in the church, there would be a greater need for discernment and revelation. God said this was needed to protect me and to know who could be trusted with the people of God, versus those who operated under their agendas. The lesson was both painful and hard, but necessary for my growth and development if I was going to be a servant in the kingdom.

CHAPTER 6

Expanding My Horizon

Now that I had learned the invaluable lesson of looking beyond the exterior of people, what they said, and how they represented themselves, it was time that I launched out into the deep and expand my horizons. It is no coincidence that whenever the Lord is about to commission his messenger, he inevitably places him or her in a season of isolation and aloneness. For it is here in the place of isolation, that God begins to shape and carve out the masterpiece that he will showcase to the world. Just think about it. Although Abraham did not completely obey God's command to leave his kindred, it wasn't until he separated from his nephew Lot, that God's divine plan for Abraham unfolded. Moses had to spend forty years on the back side of a mountain before he was ready for his encounter with Jehovah at the burning bush. After being anointed King of Israel, David had to go back to the wide-open pastures to attend his father's sheep. Paul spent three years in the desert, being taught by the "greatest teacher" before evangelizing the world. And even Jesus himself had to experience his private wilderness temptation for forty days, before his public introduction to the masses.

What is it about the experience of "isolation" that God so willingly and frequently incorporates this phenomenon into his master plan for our lives? Why does he allow us to go through seasons of aloneness? What is it about separation that brings joy to the face of God? I have come to discover that times when we are isolated, alone, and separated, are the times when we are most vulnerable to God. It is here, apart from our comfort zone, familiar family, and friends that we become open to hearing from God. It is when everything else that has been a constant in our lives, is suddenly and sometimes tragically removed and taken away, that we find ourselves in a position where we learn to become totally dependent on God. I'm not talking about trusting God through a song, a catchy phrase, or even the latest religious fad. I am talking about trusting God to the extent that he tells you to leave your job, depend on him for your sustenance, and never look back, you can do it and not even question him. It is easy to talk about trusting God when your bank account is full, or the children are all well, or the bills are all paid up. But can you trust him when the job downsizes and you're the one handed the pink slip? Can you trust God when the banker issues a repossession order and you watch as your car, your only means of transportation is being hooked up to a tow truck? Can you trust God when the mortgage or rent is way past due and you come home only to find an eviction notice posted on your door? Can you trust God when the doctor advises you it is time to call in the family? Can you trust God then?

It is in those times that God seems to do his best work. When we are at our wit's end it is then that God steps in and declares, "It's about time you turned it over to me." The scripture states in Genesis 32:24, "and Jacob was left alone." It wasn't until Jacob was "left alone," that he had his encounter with God. There he wrestled with an angel until the breaking of the day. It was not that Jacob was lonely, for he was traveling with his family, but rather he was left alone. When you look at the word *alone*, you can break it up to mean, "All One;" all one with yourself, your thoughts, your hidden struggles, and your humanity. The apostle James says that a "double-minded man is unstable in all his ways." But when you are all one, with yourself and God, only then are you in harmony with what God's destiny is for your life. "All one" signifies wholeness and singleness of purpose. Just like God placed a demand of separation and isolation on these patriarchs of the bible, the Lord spoke to me and told me to leave New Orleans and move to Houston in the summer of 1990. This was an anxious time for me, for New Orleans was the place where I was born, grew up and attended high school and college. Although my travels had afforded me to visit other cities and states, up until then, I had never established residency anywhere but in New Orleans.

In February of that same year, my mother passed away. January 25, 1990, started just like any other day until my mom became ill while at work and my eldest sister had to drive her to the hospital. Over the next few days doctors discovered that her aorta valve had torn apart and because of the extent of her hemorrhaging and elevated blood pressure, they were unable to operate. Ten days later on February 5th, after checking into the hospital, she transitioned this life to be with her Lord. Although my mother had brought all seven of her children up in the church, she backslid and left the church when I was nine years old in 1967. She remained estranged from the church for twenty years, and it was not until I accepted my first pastorate in Houma, Louisiana in 1987 that she returned to the Lord and church. During my pastoral installation service, I can recall the late Jurisdictional Bishop, Bishop J.A. Thompson, preaching the Word of God and then extending the call to discipleship to the audience. My mother stepped into the aisle, walked up to the front of the church, repented of her sins, and was restored to a relationship with Christ that very night. As a little child, I often prayed and asked God to do whatever he had to do, short of taking my mother's life, to get her back into the church. One would have speculated that being diagnosed with breast cancer a few years earlier would have been enough to get her back into the church, but not so. The remarkable miracle in all of this was that God had granted her grace for more than twenty years as she remained outside of the will of God. And yet, within three years of renewing her covenant with the Lord, God was pleased to take her into eternity with him.

As my mother lay dying in the hospital, battling with going in and out of consciousness, one minute being able to call each of her children by name, the next minute, not being able to remember or recall who any of us were; there was a period in the midst of what seemed like "endless confusion," she became lucid enough in her mind that I lead her into a prayer of repentance and confession. After reaffirming her relationship with the Lord, I shortly departed the hospital, knowing that ALL WAS WELL! Later that night, our eldest brother Henry, called to tell us that Mom had just slipped away. Initially, I felt some guilt about not being present at the time of her death, but a sense of calmness came over me, and I knew that God's will had been done. A few months after burying my mother, I sensed an urging in my spirit to leave the place of my childhood. After sharing with my wife what I believed to be the voice of the Lord giving me direction, my wife and three young children relocated to Houston with me in July of 1990. In retrospect, I realize now that the relocation to Texas was God's divine way of bringing us into a season of "all one" with him. It was befitting that Texas, also known as the *"LONESTAR"* state, is where the process of expanding my spiritual horizons began to take shape and come more fully into view.

CHAPTER 7

The Awakening

Although the state line of Texas was only three hours away from New Orleans it was a whole new world to me and my family. I initially moved to Houston first and sent for my wife and children shortly thereafter. What they say about Texas, "It is a state where everything is big," seemed to smack me right in the face. One of the first things I noticed about churches in Texas was that church buildings resembled churches and not storefronts. In Louisiana, many of the local ministries were comfortable with worshipping in small, cramped, and often unattractive spaces they liked to call sanctuaries. Now before you get started rebuking me, I understand that a building does not constitute "the church." However, the scenario of collective worshipping had taken on a life of itself in the mindset of many of the local assemblies in New Orleans. For many of the churches I knew, it did not matter how long the church's building fund had been in effect or how much money had been raised during the annual church anniversary, there never seemed to be any real significant improvements to the building itself. Maybe a few new potted plants had been placed in front of the pulpit or a coat of fresh paint applied, but never any real structural or aesthetic changes had taken place.

When we moved to Texas, I was shocked to see the saints worshipping in splendid and grand cathedrals. In

Houston alone, I was impressed to see such large and beautiful sanctuaries as Woodard's Cathedral William's Temple, Emmanuel, and Law Memorial Churches of God In Christ. I had seen churches like these populate other denominations but not COGIC. In some parts of the Church of God In Christ, a mentality existed that said, "The poorer you were, the closer to God you were." I believed this thinking permeated the mentality of the people to the extent that the buildings we worshipped in reflected what we thought was representative of our walk with God.

With the much larger, more elaborate, and spectacular houses of worship in Texas, it was a new awakening for me. Not only did I come to see what the people of God could accomplish if they worked together, but it birthed in me a new mindset, that God's people deserved the *best*. Most of the COGIC churches that resembled what I saw in Texas were on television and were in the northern and western parts of the country. My experiences were filtered through the eyes of prominent leaders who made public comments such as the one I heard at a funeral for one of the church's members while still residing in Louisiana. Doing his eulogy, the pastor boldly announced that he believed "People in the south lived closer to the Lord than people in the west and the north." This statement was made despite many of the deceased's family members sitting in the audience being from a northern state. As a result of hearing this kind of teaching for many years, my perspective had come to view churches in other parts of the country though larger, the people were not as saved as we southerners were. As a result of my warped thinking, I had come to equate the size of a church to its commitment to whether "true holiness" was that ministry's foundational teaching. In my mind the smaller the church, the godlier the people. Talk about the awakening I had when I discovered that God's Spirit dwelled in larger churches also! It was not until much later in my life I realized that this kind of teaching and rhetoric was used by many leaders as a way to justify their lack of vision and ministry shortcomings.

Not only were the church facilities in Houston more conducive to worship but also the mindset of the people was so much more expansive when it came to what it meant to be total ministry. Outside of probably two or three COGIC churches in New Orleans that were progressive, you could go to nearly any COGIC church in Houston and find people who were not married to the old traditions of the church. Women were coming to church dressed in casual attire – including wearing pants, I will talk about that later, praise and worship were the order of the day, and churches had active ongoing ministries that were actively engaged in their local communities. In Texas, it was about ministering to the whole man, educationally, economically, physically, relationally, emotionally, and spiritually. In Louisiana, most of what I experienced as worship, appeared to be only concerned with "having church."

God began conceptually dealing with me during this time. I began to see, although somewhat dimly, a light that pointed toward real ministry. Let me pause here and point out what I mean by real ministry. What I had been exposed to as a child and young adult growing up was "church" in its religious form. We knew how to praise the Lord, sing, shout, raise money, attend all the conventions, and for the most part, live holy. We had mastered the art of testimony service, where one would stand up during devotional service and tell what mighty acts the lord had done for them. The problem with testifying soon became evident as members used that time and platform to showcase their singing or speaking talent, brag about what they had been blessed with, "throw off" on other members they did not like, or spend more time praising the pastor or blaming the devil, than giving honor to God. The typical testimony in our church sounded something like this, *"first giving honor to God, who is the head of my life; second to the pastor and his wife, to the Elders and ministers, to the mothers, deacons, saints, and friends. I thank the Lord for being saved, sanctified, and filled with the Holy Ghost and a mighty burning fire. I thank God for waking me up this morning clothed in my right mind, with the activities of my limbs and a reasonable portion of health and strength. I realize that he didn't have to do it, but he did, and I'm glad about it. You know saints, the devil has been on my track and he's been trying to turn me back. I went to work today, and the devil got into my boss. People were talking about me, and I just went into my prayer closet and told God about it. You know Pastor, every time the devil gets to acting up, I just go to praying and telling that old devil, Satan, the Lord rebuke you. By the time I got home, I was so tired. The children were acting up, the house was in a mess, nothing had been done as I said, and I started rebuking the devil again. Before you knew it, everything started to get right. I thank God for our pastor because he teaches us the truth. He doesn't spare the rod when it comes to telling us what God says. And his wife is such a blessing to the church. Anything that she can do, she'll go out of her way to help you. I came to church tonight, I had to press my way to get here, but I'm here in Jesus's name. That old car was acting up and I thought I was going to get a little rest, but before I knew it, it was time for church. I desire those of you who know the words of prayer, to pray my strength in the Lord."*

Now I know some of you might be thinking or saying I am exaggerating. To be perfectly honest with you, this is a pretty "light" testimony. I mean I have heard some testimonies go on and on and on until the person in charge of devotional service had to either sing a song, hold up a bible, or stand up to get the person to cut their testimony off and sit down. One of our practices was if testimony service was going on for too long, the conductor of the service would announce at one point, that no one else stand. This was church but it was not ministry! This kind of testimony did not minister to you, let alone anyone else. One of the differences between Louisiana and Texas ministries was an emphasis on praise and worship. For a long time, I made fun of the way contemporary white churches praised the Lord. I would see them with their hands lifted, moving from side to side, usually off-beat with the music, and I would think how foolish these people looked. I mean, after all, no one could praise the Lord like the "black church." We could out sing anybody, we had the best musicians, and we could jump in the air, kick our legs from side to side, spin around, and still be on beat. So, to see saints in Houston participating in a different kind of praise and worship was at first shocking to me. But as time passed, I began to note something refreshing and inviting about this mode of praising the Lord. Praising God in this fashion made you want to remain in the presence of the Lord. Upon closer reflection, what I had become accustomed to for many years was centered on emotionalism, whereas this "new" way centered on relationship.

It was the "putting on of a new face," to an old way of doing things. It was as if I had left the dark ages and stepped right into the 21st century. It was like moving from the "alley" to the "boulevard" of religion. Church had become "modernized" and contemporary to me and I was no longer ashamed of some of the thing's church had represented. Back home there were times I felt ashamed, not of the Lord, but of inviting my unsaved friends to the local church. Some of my embarrassment was due to the physical condition of the building itself, but frequently it was because of the "backward" way we operated. This was evident in everything from preachers who could not form a grammatically correct sentence, to giant holes in walls or taped over broken windows. I frequently thought, how could I convince someone to believe in the God I serve, when the God I serve was presented as an impoverished and unintelligent deity? I know there are some of you who condemn me and have punched my ticket already to hell for being ashamed of my environment. I can hear you saying, "to be content with whatever state I find myself in." But I had always heard about this God who could take you from the dunghill and set you among princes. My grandmother always talked about God being rich, and the cattle on a thousand hills belonged to him. But for me, I did not grasp the concept of God's people being blessed in every area of their lives. Blessed in church, but not in your careers; blessed to pray, but not knowing how to speak the kings' English; blessed to dance and shout, but not to be creative in writing books; blessed to travel from local church to church, but not to minister in foreign lands; blessed to be a preacher or missionary, but not a lawyer or an engineer. No, it was not that I did not believe in the blessings of the Lord, to the contrary I did. I just did not believe as a result of what I saw that God's blessings could be so universal and all-encompassing.

It was this awakening that began to challenge me to another level in ministry and my relationship with God. I was awakened to a new way of doing things in the kingdom, a way that allowed more people to become exposed to the gospel and the message of Jesus Christ. Truth be told, some people will not venture into certain neighborhoods or enter some church buildings simply because of the location and what the facility looks like, no matter how much God is there! But when you allow God to be glorified through your worship and presentation of him as Lord, then you allow the door to be open to people from all cultures and socio-economic backgrounds.

So, this became my challenge. To move from what was, what I had been exposed to all my young life, to what I now observed before me was a better representation of what "the church" should represent. And let me tell you it was not an easy process. You would think that anyone with a shred of common sense would want to move in that direction. Easier said than done! When you have been brought up in a particular mindset, or nurtured in tradition, you fall victim to what I like to call a "pharisaical culture." This is simply doing things the same way, over and over, because this is the way our fathers did it. "And by God, if it was good enough for our fathers, then it is good enough for us!"

CHAPTER 8

Delivered From Denominations

I can recall two particular events that occurred while I was living in Houston that propelled me into a new trajectory in understanding what true ministry is about. The first thing that had a profound impact on my life was my enrollment in the Charles Harrison Mason Bible College. Once enrolled in the Bible College my mindset began to change significantly. The exposure to this environment became the incubator for my deliverance from the spirit of denominationalism.

The C.H. Mason Bible College was hosted at the Williams Temple Woodard Cathedral Church of God in Christ. It was there I had my first introduction to Professor Willie Moore. Professor Moore was a minister at the host church and unlike anyone I had ever met before. He was brash, wild, eccentric at times, but brutal in his honesty. It was not unusual for the class to see him standing on top of a desk, throwing a book, or yelling at the top of his voice. There were a couple of occasions when he became so loud and intense that professors from other classes would stop instructing their classes and peek into our room, just to make sure everyone was okay. I am sure it must have sounded as if a bomb had exploded, and Professor Moore's class had been swept away.

Dr. Moore caused me to re-evaluate my blind submission to the authority of any denomination as it related to following the church at any cost. "If they want to put me out...let them put me out," was one of the sayings he frequently could be heard shouting. He would emphasize to the students that they cannot put you out of the church, because YOU ARE THE CHURCH, and the church does not belong to them. No earthly man owned the church or died for the church, thus his lack of hesitation when it came to choosing between God and man. This man made me think of the church, not as an organization but as an organism, for the very first time. His presentation of the gospel helped peel away so many layers of denominationalism that had come to blind me to what having a relationship with God was all about. And as the layers began to fall from my eyes, I did not like what I began to see.

What I had become was a mere soldier, a puppet, and an extension of some man's empire. But what I was missing out on was being in a place where I allowed God to be God in my life. Oh, I always wanted God to be God in my life. What I did not know was that I was limiting him to the confines of my denomination. I knew our reformation taught and practiced living a holy life. I knew you could get to heaven from this church. I knew the doctrine of the church was founded and established on the bible and the Word of God. But what was I missing? What if God wanted to be God in my life "Outside" of the confines of a particular denomination? What if God wanted to do a "new" thing in my life? What if God was calling me to another area of ministry where the name on the church marquee was not as important as the name that was being lifted up inside the sanctuary? What if God wanted me to minister to a people and not a denomination? This was one of the pieces in my puzzle of destiny that was missing. Jesus was calling me, not to church ministry, but to kingdom ministry. At the time I did not fully recognize it but as time passed by, it was as if a heavy fog was slowly lifting, and I was beginning to have a clearer vision of the work the Lord was doing in me. This reminded me of St. Mark 8:24, after being touched by Jesus a blind man declared, "I see men as trees." Although the blind man began to see, his vision was still not clear, still not accurate. It was not until Jesus touched the same man a second time, that he went away seeing clearly. I confess I did not see clearly as of yet, my vision was still blurred, but my sight was on its way.

Having blurred vision at that time was part of God's plan of teaching me a valuable lesson. Before meeting Professor Moore, I was blinded to God's purpose for my life. I had vision but my vision was covered with the glaucoma of "the tenets of the spirit of religion." I could see but my sight suffered from the cataracts of the "commandments of men." I had perception but my perception was rooted in what others saw for me, and not necessarily what I saw for myself.

One day I was having trouble reading something with my eyeglasses on. When I removed my glasses to attempt to finish reading the document, I was astonished the words on the page were much clearer without my glasses. For a moment I thought that maybe the Lord had healed my eyes and the corrective lenses I needed to wear for the last thirty-five years would be a thing of the past. A few days later I went to the optometrist to have my vision checked. I discovered that because of my aging process, bifocals were necessary. The interesting thing I learned about bifocals was that you use a different part of the lens, the top, middle, and bottom, to see objects that are at a far, medium, or close distance. Certain parts of the lens are specifically designed to address certain vision deficiencies in the eyes. If you need to see an object that is far away and utilize the wrong portion of the lens to look through, you will not get an accurate picture of what you desire to see, despite having glasses on. But to see the object clearly and without flaws, you must look through the appropriate section of the single lens. Even though the glass is a single lens, it has been manufactured to provide a valuable service in a multiplicity of uses. The same lens, but many different uses. The same lens but now the ability to see objects from differing perspectives. No longer the "one size fits all."

What I had been doing was looking through the wrong portion of the lens. My vision was limited and what I was using as corrective lenses was the "sight of men" and not of God. It was not that God had not shown some things to me regarding my future, for he had. At this stage in my life, I had got to a point where I subconsciously believed it would be God using men to open the doors of my destiny, and not God himself. But as I look back over my life and recognize the hand of God, I now know that what God had for me, no flesh and blood could get the glory. Where I was going, *HE* would lead the way. The things he needed to tell me he would not trust to any man, but the Lord himself would speak to me. Many years later he would tell me **"I didn't forget how to talk, you forgot how to listen."**

It was through the exploits of Professor Moore that I began to hear the voice of God concerning the kingdom. He was a man of unorthodox ways and teaching style, but he was apt to get your attention and challenge you to think outside the box. He forced me to take an introspective look at myself, who I was, and where I was going. Then he dared to challenge me to get to that place even if it meant going against the status quo. Without a doubt, he recognized something in me that I could not discern for myself.

For me, initiating significant change would be a challenge, because it had been instilled within me to always be a "team player." One of my former pastor's definitions of fellowship was, "all the fellows in one ship." Although this may be a simple saying, it carries a profound message regarding getting along with others on the team, no matter the personal cost. Although I always thought of myself as a team player, I was usually the one who would buck the system. I was the one who always delivered a word of challenge or correction to the Body. I did not know then, but I do know now, that was God's way of nudging me in the direction he had destined for me to go.

Nevertheless, I would still find myself wanting to be "one of the boys." I always had a longing to fit in and be a part of the in-crowd. But as I would painfully learn over the next few years, God had called not only myself, but my wife Elleanor, my daughters Keosha and Courtney, and my son George Jr., to go against the grain. We would ultimately walk in a place of isolation from men, to be used by God. This was a cost at one time I did not want to pay. I would find myself bargaining with God over the next few years, negotiating a settlement on being able to walk in destiny and yet fit in. After all, I had watched others over the years who appeared to have mastered that art and were doing rather nicely. But what I did not comprehend then, was that the map that God had laid out for me, was custom fitted to my anointing. So, what worked for others would be null and void when it came to me.

Just ask David the shepherd boy, in 1 Samuel 17:39, when King Saul offered him his armor to fight the giant Goliath. David refused the request stating, "I cannot go with these; for I have not proved them." So, David faced the giant, not with another man's covering, but with the unique tools he felt most confident and comfortable with – a sling and five smooth stones. David accepted the challenge and prevailed because he was willing to forego precautions and customary measures and trust in the God of "Something Different."

The second incident occurred also in Houston and as I reflect on it now, I see the same kind of brashness that

Professor Moore would have reveled in. I was an associate elder at a particular church, and a fellow minister was sponsoring a special service. One of the special guests would be the choir from his hometown church. During the days of preparation leading up to the event, I was asked to serve as Master of Services to ensure the flow of service was at its maximum effectiveness. The Lord had placed an anointing on my life in the ministry of praise and worship. Normally I would have agreed to serve in this capacity because I was a team player. But a month or so before this time, the choir from my local church back in Louisiana was on tour, and my wife and I had arranged for them to minister during one of our local services. This same minister had caused so much trouble and turmoil regarding showing hospitality to my church choir and voiced his concerns regarding not seeding any monetary gifts towards them. The choir from my former church came and ministered to the congregation and many people were blessed, delivered, and gave their lives to Christ that night. Well, the other Elder observed the impact the service had on the congregation, organized another service, and invited the local choir to minister. At first, he had someone else ask me to conduct the service. After he heard that I declined, he approached me himself and inquired whether I was going to be in charge of the services. This was the first time in my life that I refused to do what was asked of me in a church service. Now you may say that I was wrong and that I should have overlooked this injustice and allowed God to handle the situation. Yes, yes, I hear you saying, "Vengeance is mine,

I will repay, saith the Lord." And you may be very well right. But what took place was a literal transformation in my character and mode of operation. All along I had been the person everyone could count on to "support their program." Some would say, "You can always count on Elder Montgomery."

But right then, I was presented with the situation of going along with the program or bucking the system. Bucking the system was not an easy thing for me to do. To buck the system, leaders would label you as a maverick, a renegade, and a hothead. To those in authority, this kind of action would place you on the front line for ridicule, scorn, and being "passed over" for key positions. Initially, I thought about swallowing my hurt feelings and going ahead and acquiescing to the request from my co-laborer in ministry. I thought to myself, "Do it this time and another opportunity would present itself." I tried to convince myself to go ahead, but for now, ultimately things would work out.

But overriding the "all is well" response cascading from my friends' lips, was a boldness to make a stand, Here and Now! What better place to make a stand than in the church? I repeated my denial of participating as Master of Services for the program and, word of my actions spread quicker than a rumor from a gossiper's lips. On the night of the program, my wife and I attended the service and sat in the balcony of the church. Services went on but it was evident that the atmosphere was not conducive to the flow of the Spirit. It was as if everyone was trying too hard to manufacture the presence of the Lord when all they had to do was invite him in. The services were doomed from the start because the spirit of "SELF" was on display and not God.

As I sat in my seat, I asked God to forgive me if my actions became a stumbling block to anyone aware of the situation. But God gave me peace of spirit and an assurance that he was pleased with me because I had taken a stand against "church as usual." In the long run, people recognized what I did was right, and many came to me afterward and supported me in my actions. I grieved that many persons who came to the services that night left with unfulfilled needs. But I felt secure in that my motives were consistent with the character of the God of the Bible. For God did say, "I also will laugh at your calamity; I will mock when your fear cometh," Proverbs 1:26. My action did not score many brownie points for me with those in authority. It did however reveal something about myself that I had come to accept as part of my character, and that was, that I would no longer would be satisfied or comfortable with just going through the motions to satisfy people. I was not quite sure where this "something" was taking me, but I knew that I would never again feel like "one of the guys." It is like once you cross over that line, you can never go back again. This was a huge cost to pay and at the time I did not fully understand the price it would cost me. I would come to discover years later the cost of my stand.

CHAPTER 9

I Hear Trumpets!

Unbeknownst to me at the time but relocating to Houston was part of God's plan for my growth process. Upon reflection, moving away from what was familiar to me, was the Lord's way of maturing me in that season of my life. Several years later I found myself contemplating returning home after the unexpected death of my grandmother. My wife's parents were getting up in age and both of us sensed a need to be closer to family. I telephoned my former pastor back home and shared with him my feelings about returning home and some of my experiences in Texas. While still residing in Houston, I had been presented with a choice to pastor either one of two churches in Texas. One of the churches was in a rural area south of Houston while the other ministry was in the city of Houston itself. I called back home to discuss these options with my former pastor expecting some pearls of wisdom and possible guidance. What I heard were words quite the opposite, along with a sense of not being welcomed back home. I must admit that this was a tremendous blow to me for I thought I would be welcomed back with open arms. It felt more like a door had been slammed in my face and the curtains drawn closed. I began to feel like a vagabond with no place to go. I was feeling the need to be closer to our families back in Louisiana, but I did not feel welcomed back home by "the church." So, I sought the Lord for direction as God continued to order my steps. I accepted the pastorate of the church in the country and the Lord began teaching me how to serve his people. Although I learned so much while shepherding this wonderful congregation, I knew from the beginning this was a place of transition for both myself as well as the local assembly. The former church's minister decided to start up a ministry in the city of Houston and the church was left without a pastor. Upon accepting the leadership of the church, the Lord continued the work he had already begun in me. Being one of the youngest pastors in the area, often placed me in a position where I found myself challenging the mindset of the "religious authorities" and ministries of the area. I began preaching the gospel that condemned "shacking up," adultery, gambling, backbiting, hating your brother, and the like. It was as if people had never heard the gospel before. More people began coming to the church and lives were being changed. The spiritual leadership of the community was not pleased. Part of their displeasure centered on them being exposed for who they really were and the fact that many of their members were leaving their church to attend ours.

The Lord blessed the ministry to quadruple in growth in two years. Between my second and third year of pastoring the Evangelist Temple Church of God in Christ, I sensed an unction from the Lord, it was time to return to New Orleans. The company I was working for at the time had a position open up in a suburb of New Orleans and I was asked if I would be willing to relocate back to

New Orleans and take the job. Although my employer was unaware, I had asked the Lord in prayer if going back home was his will for me, that he would confirm it by opening a door so I would be able to financially support my family. I began making plans to return home and resigned from my pastorate. The members refused to accept my resignation and recommended I stay on as their pastor, commuting between Bay City, Texas, and New Orleans every other week. I continued to serve as the church's pastor for six months traveling up and down Interstate 1-10 until I explained to the members, that they needed a full-time pastor who was available to serve the congregation as it deserved. These were God's people, the same people who had accepted and embraced me and my family, and I was feeling as if I was "short-changing" them by giving them half a month's worth of pastoral leadership. I knew that in some rural churches, it was customary for the pastor to be present twice out of the month on Sundays. But this was not my philosophy, and I believed the members needed someone who could be totally dedicated to them in their time as well as their support if they were to continue to grow spiritually. And so, I asked again, and this time was released by the membership from the mantle of a chief shepherd.

The Lord orchestrated my return to New Orleans seven and a half years after initially leading me and my family to Houston. I recalled the conversation I had with my former pastor two years earlier, and when my secular job officially moved us back home, everyone back home expected me to fall right back in line and reunite with my former church. Well, to everyone's surprise, my family and I united with one of the denomination's most progressive, innovative, and contemporary ministries in the city. This was a shock to everyone. Here I was, a staunch supporter and team member, going over to the "other side." You must understand that although this ministry was of the same denomination and fellowshipped with my former church, they were looked upon and branded as being "unsaved". This ministry was the talk of the town and because it was "fresh" and inspiring to many young people, others who were envious, often engaged in good old-fashioned "Hate-o-rade." The motto was not, "If you can't beat them join them," it was more, "if you can't beat them discredit them." So, there was a consistent attempt to discredit this ministry and its leadership in every sense of the word.

The move that my family and I made was viewed as a betrayal of sorts by my former pastor and church. But I could not allow what God had begun to do in me to be contaminated by the vestiges of past relationships and connections that had been put to death. God had begun to open my eyes during my tenure in Texas. He exposed me to a different mindset, different people, and a different culture. I was determined not to allow all that God had poured into me to leak out to please man. Before I left Texas, the Lord directed me where to serve and had already prepared the heart of the pastor to whom I would submit. Upon our arrival back to New Orleans, our family was welcomed with open arms by this ministry, The Full Gospel Church of God In Christ, and then, Pastor Charles E. Brown.

This ministry soon became a major building block to my overall spiritual development and growth. I had been strategically planted in this ministry to learn about new and innovative ways of working in the kingdom. The mindset of Pastor Brown and Full Gospel ministry closely mirrored what I had been exposed to in Texas. The pastor believed in and practiced excellence in ministry. It may sound quite absurd, but I discovered a pastor who believed in training the leadership of the church for service. I had never been a part of a church where the pastor would have members of the clergy, ushers, and others involved in serving the Eucharist, practicing and rehearsing every aspect of the service, including walking in, where someone would stand, how to serve the people, and so forth. That just blew my mind the first time I saw that. And if you were late arriving for "rehearsal," then you did not participate and could not serve during that service. I began to soak up everything I could from this awesome man of God. Focusing on members being present and services starting on time, displaying an orderly flow of services and meetings, conducting church business in a professional and business-like manner, and learning to celebrate others in a first-class manner became the paradigm shift that I found absent in my earlier ministry stint in New Orleans. It was as if I was the canvas and the image I had been painted before, was now being painted over and a new sense of being, a new sense of purpose and ministry was being revealed. And for the first time,

I found a leader who was not intimated by the giftings of others. This was something I had never experienced before. Every leader I had served with before now, had problems embracing what God was doing in my life. They often spent more time pointing out that they had a bigger church, they raised more money, or they had a better ministry than everyone else. Remarks such as, "We built our new church first" or "Our people are number one in giving," always lent themselves to competition among local ministries. And if the truth is told, what all the talk amounted to was being a "big fish in a little pond." If these same pastors had taken the time to expand their vision, they would have seen that although they were building bigger facilities, they were doing so with enormous debt. Although they were raising large offerings, people never saw the result of their giving materialize toward kingdom goals. Instead of saving more souls they often boasted of fancier cars, more expensive suits, and more lavish homes. Meanwhile, other ministries were building church edifices debt-free. They were ministering to the needs of the community by way of food pantries, homeless shelters, unwed mothers, drug addiction programs, and school and tutorial programs that I had not seen our churches commit to.

This church however was on the cutting edge of ministry. The pastor had taken the time to invest in his leaders and members, the essence of what the kingdom was about. Here was a man that did not focus his attention on what everyone else was doing, but rather on what God had assigned him to do. This pastor knew who he was in God and could care less about how great or gifted anyone else was in preaching, evangelizing, or prophesying. This was the first pastor I had been under who sought out the various ministry gifts in the body of Christ as a way of building up his local and jurisdictional parishioners. So many times, I observed pastors who almost to a fault, would keep their members sheltered from other major voices of the kingdom to keep the people "reserved" to themselves. It was one thing to teach your members about not running to every crusade, camp meeting, or revival to protect them from exposing themselves to every wind and doctrine. But what some pastors were doing was to keep their flocks isolated and apart from others and look to "them only" as the panacea for their life issues. But this pastor understood Ephesians 4:11 when God gave the five-fold gifts in the church for the "edifying of the body of Christ and work of the ministry." I would hope every pastor and leader understood that you cannot do it alone, even if all the five gifts are operational in your own life. You need others to reach out to those whom you are not called to and will never come into personal contact with.

I enrolled and took part in a school of ministry that had been started by my pastor. I served as one of the school's first instructors, teaching Old Testament Survey. Under this pastor, I began to absorb and truly grasp foundational principles about "EXCELLENCE" in ministry. Going through the motions was not enough for this pastor. Sitting under this ministry enhanced the spirit of Excellence that God had already birthed within me and was now taking me to an even higher level of spiritual operation. Ministry was not something you did on Sundays or mid-week service, but if done right, it is an everyday part of one's vocabulary, character, and way of doing things.

It is sad to say what should have been "common practice" for the body of Christ was missing. Here we are testifying to serving a God of greatness, excellence, and order, while at the same time offering him a plate of cold, uninspiring, repetitive, and stale worship. Starting services on time should not be the exception, but rather the norm. And starting services with 10% of the congregation present is even more of an indictment of the ministry. What if you arrived to work late 90% of the time? What do you think would happen? Now think of God as your employer and guess what he would do with those who habitually are late in getting into his presence? So, boasting that "we start our service on time," is meaningless if no one is there but you and the musician. A good pastor friend of mine once said he requires his leaders to be early, for "when you're early you're really on time; but when you're on time, you're late." Spending time in worship touching the heart of God should be our aim instead of rushing through worship to get to the next item on the program. Even sowing seeds of our finances should be conducted with integrity and expectation, as opposed to making people feel guilty and condemned if they don't have to give. I have been in some services where you were sowing your seed, and the person facilitating the offering would publicly announce your name and the exact amount of what you had given. I have been in services where ushers were told to stand in front of exits and keep anyone from leaving during offering services. Choirs were asked to minister to the congregation with little or no rehearsal time. Preachers and teachers ministered the Word of God with no preparation. This is not Excellence, this is a "that will do" mentality. The thought by some leaders was that people would go along with the program if you got them shouting and dancing. Get them caught up in their emotions and they will not be able to distinguish true glory from superficial, artificial, and manufactured praise. And what many of our churches, denominations, ministries, and pastors have done is substitute the anointing which comes fresh from the altar, with yesterday's leftovers from glories past. Well, I do not know about you, but I am tired of hearing another message that someone copied off of a compact disc, YouTube, or television program. I am tired of hearing a message that the speaker heard from another place he had been and decided that if it worked for that place, then why not duplicate it in this place? I need a TODAY word from the Lord that will minister to me right where I AM. And although Bishop Charles E. Blake, Prophetess Juanita Bynum, or Bishop T.D. Jakes preached that same word last week because God is a progressive and always moving God, that word that was spoken then, may not be the word that the Lord has designed for my life today. If God's mercies are "new" every morning, could it be that the Lord has a "fresh and proceeding word" that is tailor-made for you, just for this day?

During my three-year tenure at that ministry, the pastor preached a series of messages entitled, "I Hear Trumpets," that tied into the Old Testament Year of Jubilee celebration. The series focused on identifying who you were in God and your right to a King's inheritance. The message that the pastor imparted to us first empowered us to identify our rightful place in the kingdom; second, it helped us to recognize our kinship and connection to the Father; and finally, it taught us how to access the keys to the kingdom. "I hear trumpets" became more than a slogan, it became our battle cry. It infused us with a passion and determination to strive for the best that God has to offer us. If we are the King's kids, then we ought to look the best, eat the best, drive the best, and live the best. Indeed, we ought to look like kings' kids. Proverbs 13:22 declares that "the wealth of the sinner is laid up for the just." My pastor taught us that as a child of the king, we should *expect* the best. It is our right to expect the best education, accommodations, treatment, living conditions, and everything that goes along with it. St. Matthews 6:33 states, "But seek ye first the kingdom of God and his righteousness, and all these things shall be added unto you."

Whenever we hear a trumpet blowing, we naturally get excited. The blowing of trumpets signified that something special was about to happen. It was used to announce an event, signal a particular action such as an attack or retreat, and played parts in specific celebrations and ceremonies. To me, hearing trumpets is related to the coming of royalty or some dignitary. As for me, I am royalty not because of my natural ancestry, but because of the spiritual bloodline, I was birthed into. Because my father is a king, I inherit the status of a prince. And whenever a prince enters the room, trumpets should sound. I always knew this intellectually but never internalized it regarding myself until I became exposed to this revelatory word. I knew this was true for Bishops, Overseers, Apostles, Prophets, Superintendents, Pastors, and other great men and women of God because I observed these people living like kings. They were driving the best cars, wearing the most expensive tailor-made suits, and living in spacious mansions. But I never saw myself in that same light. My pastor's teaching challenged me to raise my expectations and caused me to begin to recognize what the Lord had predestined for me. I now recognized that trumpets were not reserved for a special class of king's children, but every one of his children. So now I began to see myself as God saw me. What I had seen as a failure, God saw as an opportunity. What I had seen as poverty, God saw as deliverance. What I had seen as small and insignificant, God saw as big and relevant. My portrait of myself was suddenly transformed into a showpiece, with God being the master artist. The astonishing thing to me was that the devil already knew who I was in the spirit. I just had not come into the knowledge of who I was. That is why the devil tried his best to keep me from finding out "WHO" I was. And just like me, he has tried to keep you from discovering who you really are. As the master of deceit, he uses distractions, emotional hurt, psychological trauma, and yes, even those closest to you to keep you from discovering the "WHO" God knows you to be. You are not just some school teacher, some laborer, some craftsman, some salesman, some student, some housewife, or some husband. You are, **"a chosen generation, a royal priesthood, a holy nation, a peculiar people,"** 1 Peter 2:9, and have been designed to house the very glory of God. You are the living, breathing, walking, and talking embodiment of the **RIGHTEOUSNESS of GOD!** He cares so much for us as his children, that he permitted us to hold *"his treasure"* in our EARTHEN VESSELS. So, go ahead let the trumpets blow, let the horns sound, and tell the world that light has invaded the dark places. Tell the devil his time is up. Tell your enemies that "no weapon that has been formed against you shall prosper." Tell those who sought to kill you, as they did me, that I am still breathing. Tell those that buried you, I will rise again. Tell the naysayer "You better recognize." Tell your past that it's just that, YOUR PAST, and I am running into my future. Tell your crooked places you have just been made straight. Tell your rough places you have just been made smooth. Tell all your hang-ups, that they have been hung up. Go ahead and blow the trumpets! Blow until weights drop off. Blow until backbiters and gossipers shut their mouths. Blow until haters must stop hating on you and give pause for celebration. Blow until your enemies take a seat at your feet. Blow until your purpose lines up with your destiny. Go ahead and sound the alarm, for **I HEAR TRUMPETS!!!**

CHAPTER 10

The Silent Killer

One of the greatest assets that a person can have is the light of ambition. Ambition is the fuel that powers the engine to success. Although a positive trait, the tools of ambition can also be used in such a negative way that it becomes a deadly liability. Unbridled and ungodly ambition will ultimately lead you down a path of destruction. Let me explain more fully. I recall some of the dreams I had as a young child where the Lord revealed certain moments in my walk with him. During many of the barren times in my life when it did not seem as though anything would work out for me, I found myself reflecting on what God had shown and spoken to me and this gave me the confidence to press forward. Since many of these things had not come to fruition yet, it became the fuel to my faith that God was not through with me.

I must confess however that there were many times when my confidence grew weak and became shaken. I often found myself in places where no matter how God anointed me, things seemed just beyond my reach. When I did all I could, and appeared to be next in line, promotion always seemed to slip between my fingers as someone else would step right in front of me. For a long time, I battled with this dilemma. Because I did not emanate from a regal religious family or possess the ancestral heritage of being the offspring of a Bishop or even a pastor, it seemed that others less spiritual leapfrogged right over me. I was great at lifting a song, exhorting the people, or even delivering an inspiring word. But when it came to what I thought mattered, which were positions and appointments, it inevitably went to the pastor's son or some other person with "connections."

I soon found myself accepting what was, as what would always be. I convinced myself at one point, that's just the way it is. I can recall talking with a person whom I looked up to who was a District Superintendent at the time. This man who had several churches under his oversight was pastoring a well-established church and was seen as quite an important figure. As we talked one day, he began to share some of his philosophy that I foolhardily bought into. He pointed out to me that he made it a personal habit of praising the Jurisdictional Bishop every chance he got. He went on to tell me that in so doing, whenever important positions or appointments would come up, the Bishop would seek out those persons who were solidly in his corner. The way the Bishop determined who was for him resided in the intensity and frequency of praise and support he received from his constituency. This all made good sense to me. I rationalized to myself that if I were in the person of authority's position, I would elevate the person who spoke well of me and had my best interests at heart. The Superintendent went on to state, "If you scratch my back, I'll scratch your is the way you get ahead in this game." I thought about what he had said later and took a retrospective look back over my life to see if what he said had any validity. I began to recall certain people who had been promoted up the ladder and others who, though gifted, remained stationary. As I took inventory, I noted that everyone who was called crazy or radical never went very far. Those were the ones who generally were not well connected, were not the offspring of prominent leaders of the church, or were not large financial givers. It was bad enough if you had been marked with one of these traits within the leadership circles, God forbid if you had two or more. They would tell me that leaders would mark you with a giant "X" on your back and no matter how the Lord would use you, your gift would not make room for you in their scenario. You would not get many; if any, opportunities to speak in church and if you did, you could rest assured the leaders would "sit on you," as you ministered. When I say, sit on you, this refers to people intentionally not supporting you verbally or with their encouragement. On the other hand, it was easy to see those who were invited into and welcomed into the church system and religious hierarchy. They usually had close kinship ties to the pastor or leader, they frequently were the most physically attractive persons, and they always were singled out for sowing that "special seed offering." Years later when I thought about it I recalled many of my contemporaries going to their parents for money or checks to seed into the offerings. Once I found myself in the financial office of a church after the offering had been received. When the finance officers got to this particular preacher's check, they simply pulled it and placed it aside. They began to laugh and said, "We got another bad check." When I asked how they knew the check was bad, they informed me that every check this particular elder wrote, was bad and they stopped depositing his checks because it was costing the church more money in non-sufficient funds fees. I asked them if the pastor had been made aware of this and they all looked at one another and almost simultaneously, in one unified voice said, "Yes he knows." The sowing of seed for this person was done in such a way as to impress others. Giving for him, like so many people became something you did for the show and not for the love of God or ministry.

The denomination that I grew up in prided itself on having "order." The Ecclesiastical Hierarchy in my church consisted of Pastors, District Superintendents, and Jurisdictional Prelates or Bishops. This hierarchy is mirrored at the district, state, and national levels of my denomination. Male Presidents and Female Chairladies over the Youth, Music, Missions, Evangelism, and Sunday School departments. These were the major auxiliaries of the church but there were others such as the Sunshine Band, Purity, Young Women's Christian Council, Bible Band, Sewing Circle, Volunteers, and Pastor's Aid, to name a few. As a church body, we were trained and taught to always bless the leader of that auxiliary. So, the local person would bless the district representative, who in turn would bless the state leader, who found themselves obligated to bless the national leader. This process was formed to create a never-ending, perpetual pyramid cycle of ensuring that whoever was at the top of the pyramid, would receive financial compensation.

If your desire, dream, or ambition was to get to the top, then that meant you being the Presiding Prelate or National Supervisor of Women for the Church of God In Christ. Understand you started at your local church being trained for church work at a young age. It would be here, in the Sunday School or Sunshine Band that you started out being indoctrinated in obeying leadership at all costs.

From childhood, you are taught that the pastor or leader is to be followed without question. Forget about being an individual, different, or unique. Fall in line and become another in the long line of "cookie cutter" saints. After all, the bible teaches us in Hebrews 13:17, "obey them that have the rule over you, and submit yourselves; for they watch for your souls." This was one of leadership's favorite scriptures to pull out and use whenever the need to manipulate a situation called for it. Believe me, obeying leadership was a focal point taught more times that I could count. So, if one had any ambitions about climbing up the ladder of denominational hierarchy, one had better adopt the philosophy of the Superintendent who told me while standing outside of a particular church one day, "Praise the leadership, and when it is your turn, they'll remember you;" or better put, "you scratch my back and I'll scratch yours."

CHAPTER 11

The Man In The Mirror

Tragically somewhere along my spiritual walk with the Lord I bought into the church's system and mindset, which I had observed so many around me operating in. Being radical and different was not the passport to acceptance into the church's network of leadership. It was about fitting in and becoming a team player. I began questioning whether this was God's path for any elevation that he had for me. I reasoned within myself, that if I made it to the top, I would have a better opportunity to affect real substantive change for many more who had been overlooked. I convinced myself that I would play the game just to get the "prize." The prize was having a position of authority inside the church world. I honestly believed at the time this could be accomplished without me "selling out." I had watched, what I felt was others selling out and it was shameful. Surely this would never happen to me, or so I thought. Everyone else could sell out but not me. After all, I had grown up in an impoverished environment, the projects of New Orleans. I did not have the privilege of being the offspring of a preacher and everything I received, I had to fight for. The path was not smooth for me but was filled with potholes, ditches, detours, roadblocks, and dead ends because of who I was. Like Elijah, I thought because I was the only one left still living a holy life, "selling out" would never be a part of my story.

I would allow myself to get caught up in the "glamour" of religion. Oh yes, there is a side of religion that is glamorous and full of stardom. This is the side that captivates the heart of some and causes them to fall in love with ministry. It is big offerings, name recognition, preaching engagements, leading a contingent of adjutants, and all the trappings that accompany stardom. Although I could not identify it then, I recognize it now as the *Spirit of the Pharisee.* Like the Pharisees, religion glorified stardom more than servanthood; it glorified the creature more than the creator; it glorified outward beauty more than inner purity, and it glorified works more than faith. It was at this place that being waited upon by others became easier and easier. If you were fortunate to get on the preaching "circuit," you knew you had made it. Want to hear a "word" that would shout the people and leave them excited, you knew which preacher to call. In need of a large financial rally, there were certain "personalities" gifted in this area as well. Because certain preachers attracted specific crowds, you could pretty much gauge who would show up based on the speaker scheduled. These followers in some circles would be called "spiritual groupies." The atmosphere of the church changed from being a place of healing into a place where networking and connecting with like-minded, upwardly mobile movers and shakers became the choice of the day. Instead of falling in love with Jesus, I like some others, had fallen in love with ministry.

Speaking engagements came as did appointments to various churches. Soon I was appointed to various key positions in the denomination. The recognition that I had sought was finally coming my way. I would be lying if I told you that I did not enjoy the acclaim and praise that came with the positions. Things were finally beginning to happen for me. People were beginning to see that I could do more than preach. People were beginning to see the exhorter and worship leader that had laid dormant inside of me. Finally, some recognition! This felt good. Maybe you have not ever been to this place, and if not, then I am glad for you. But I must be real and say that after struggling all of those years and seemingly not getting anywhere, I felt vindicated now that things were beginning to move in my ministry. I had now ascended to some very lofty places inside the denomination. It was perceived inside certain church circles, that one word from me had the power to either break or make you, or so I thought. I was one of the "rising stars" of the church and was well on my way.

But how many of you know that when God has a calling on your life, the Lord will not allow you to stray too far off course before he decides to reel you back in? I honestly do not believe that the Lord enjoys humbling us, but I do know that he will ultimately get the glory. Just when you feel everything is coming together, God in his grace, will pull everything apart and turn your world upside down. It is when you feel on top of the mountain that God delights in showing you, *"You're not all that."* Whenever you get too big for God to use, he has a way of bringing you back down to size and letting you know that without him, you can do nothing. I know now that when you are down and out, have hit rock bottom and there is no place else to go, God in his infinite wisdom has you in the perfect place where he has your undivided attention.

Have you ever noticed someone drowning in a body of water? They reach up to anything that might assist them with saving their lives. A drowning person is not concerned with the color, gender, or makeup of what it is that will save him or her. They are only concerned with getting help because they understand that they are near the point of death. Before getting to that point, it is much more difficult to see the need for help. I mean things are going well and you are living the life. I believe it is at this point of "mountain top" living where Satan does his most damage to the people of God. 1 Corinthians 10:12 admonishes us, "Wherefore let him that thinketh he standeth take heed lest he fall." One of Satan's tricks is to get you to a place where you feel you are invincible. "Pride goeth before destruction, and a haughty spirit before a fall," is the lesson to be learned from Proverbs 16:18. Once, I remember preaching a message entitled, "Be Careful of Mountaintop Experiences." Most people think the most dangerous position to be in is when you are broke, busted, and disgusted. I agree that turbulent times and conditions such as these are most uncomfortable, and no one enjoys being in that place. But strangely enough, those are the times that often force us to our knees and in the presence of the Almighty. We have seen it manifested time and again, that when we have been most challenged as an individual, church, or nation we come together in prayer, unified in one purpose, despite our differences. However contrary to popular opinion, I contend that it is not at our lowest point, but at our highest peak, or mountaintop victories, that the enemy finds us most vulnerable. Human nature tells us it is okay to let our guards down and relax once we have made it to the top. **You have made it! Job Well done! Take a breather**! At that precise moment when we choose to relax and become "Eased in Zion," the enemy usurps that opportunity to search for a chink in our armor, a breach in our spiritual walls, and very quietly and discreetly, slips in and wreaks havoc in our lives. It was NOT when David was the boy shepherd facing his Goliath that he was most vulnerable to Satan's attacks. I contend it was after David had slain the giant and later became King, that Satan took the opportunity to destroy him. David's fall came after succumbing to his flesh, entering into an adulterous relationship with Bath-Sheba, and having her husband placed on the front line of the battle so he might be killed. Satan always will bide his time for what comes AFTER mountaintop victories.

Like King David, when I thought I had it going on, the Lord began to deal with me. He took me through a Prodigal Son experience so I could begin to "come to myself." It was as if I was beholding my image in a mirror. The longer I looked in the mirror, the more I saw a person I did not even know. The man in the mirror I saw looked like me, but this could not be me. The closer I looked, the more I disliked what I saw. Yes, I was riding high and climbing the proverbial ladder, but I could sense that something was not quite right. Something was missing, something that was not quite the same. The Lord was still using me to preach, teach, win souls to Christ, and work in ministry, but I could not shake the feeling that there had to be something more than this; something more than just going to church; something more than a good feeling; something more than church as usual. When I took a closer look at what I was becoming and where I was heading, I began to see that instead of becoming what God wanted me to become, I had assimilated into what the politics of religion said I had to be to get ahead.

What church was mandating and what God wanted from me were two distinct and radically different things. Somewhere along the way, I had lost the innocence of my youth. The gospel that God had called and commissioned me to preach had become influenced and tainted by the cunning craftiness of men. Lost in the fog of church work and politics was a person who had once been on fire for the Lord and unwilling to compromise his ethics and values. I had somehow allowed myself to become "star-struck" by the grandeur of the bright lights of Christianity. What I saw NOW did not measure up to what God had previously revealed to me. Like Simon Peter, I had taken my eyes off Jesus and refocused them on Bishops, Pastors, and Evangelists as my measuring stick. The vision of where the Lord was taking me had been replaced by the reality of where I was. I had given over the authority of my life to religion and religious people. Did I blame myself for my shortcomings? Did I accept responsibility for my actions in handing over the keys to my life? Did I acknowledge that it was nobody else's fault but mine? Initially, my responses to such inquiries were all No. However, as I began to mature in the faith and looked in the mirror of my soul, I saw a clear reflection of myself. I did not see any pastor, bishop, or another church member. I see now that God gives each of us the power of choice, and unfortunately, I made more than my share of bad ones. I had to come to a place after prayerfully searching my heart and begging the Lord for forgiveness and grace, where I began accepting responsibility for my actions. It was not the actions of anybody else that caused me to become disfigured in the sight of God. It was ALL ME!

While acknowledging my failures, I need to point to the role that the church plays in the development of the believer. It is primarily through our families and church environment that most of us are initially exposed to the ways of the Lord. Our life's personal experiences help shape our view of who the Lord is. Fortunately, or unfortunately, that view is frequently framed by individuals who stand as representatives of the Body of Christ. What an indictment of the church when those who should be mentoring and molding the lives of others in a positive framework, abuse that sacred privilege to paint negative images on the souls of young Christians. The church must be willing to look at ourselves in the mirror and honestly assess what we have become. And it is not until we can truthfully acknowledge our shortcomings and seek divine forgiveness, that we can reposition ourselves to becoming "the righteousness of God."

CHAPTER 12

Following The Cloud

Taking an introspective look at how far he had fallen, the prodigal son cried out in St. Luke 15:18 and said, "I will arise and go to my father, and will say unto him, Father, I have sinned against heaven, and before thee." He understood that if he was going to survive, he had to move from the place of his now to the place of his destiny. His relocation was more than a physical transference from one place to another; it was a relocation of his mind, his heart, his dreams, and his passion. To stay where he was surely meant death; if not physically, certainly it meant the death of his self-esteem, his aspirations, his hopes, and his relationship with his family. Like the prodigal, I too got caught up in something that would have swallowed me up and devoured me. And just like the prodigal, I heard the voice of the Lord when he broke through my pain and spoke to my destiny.

My family and I were living in Slidell, Louisiana, a suburb of New Orleans when some of our friends dropped by for a visit. A minister and his wife had brought along one of their friends I had met before, but up to that point, had not gotten to know very well. While my wife was sharing with our friends, the young man asked me to walk with him outside. While gazing into a star-filled sky, this young man began prophesying to me. He told me that my family and I would soon be leaving our home church and relocating out of state. He went on to tell me that once we relocated, we would find ourselves at a ministry that would recognize the calling in us. But he added that it was needful for my wife and me to just sit for a season. He went on to share with me that both my wife and I had been deeply wounded in ministry but God was moving us to a place of healing. Finally, he admonished me not to get involved in ministry right away. He instructed me not to accept any ministry positions and to just **Sit Still** and allow the Lord to Heal us. Well, the first thing that came to my mind was the fact that there was this "youngster," nearly half my age, prophesying to me. Did he not know who I was? I could sense in myself a spirit of pride and arrogance beginning to rise in me. I quickly caught myself and bringing myself under subjection, told him I did not know where this was coming from. I went on to explain to him that we were happy at our present ministry and that things could not be better. I assured him that I had my fill of pastoring and had recently just turned down a pastorate in the city where I lived. I smugly announced to him that I would pray about the "word" he had just given me and see what the Lord had to say. He agreed that I should consult the Lord and simply smiled.

It did not take God long to start "troubling the water." When the Lord is ready for you to move, he always has a way of making the comfortable become uncomfortable. After being employed with the same company for three years, I had come to a place in my career where I felt very competent and performed my job quite well. The ministry that had previously met my spiritual needs suddenly left me with a hunger that could not be fulfilled. The comfort of family and friends that was supportive of me, began to wane, and felt so distant now. Something strange was happening to me and I could not quite explain what I was feeling. What comforted me, now left me feeling empty. What once fulfilled me, now left me unsatisfied. What I once found endearing, I was now ready to walk away from. I did not know it at the time, but this was God's way of getting me out of my comfort zone and to the place where I could hear from him. I began to sense in my spirit an urging for a greater challenge. Reflecting on that season in my life, everything had become so easy and routine for me and that is never the best place to be. Remember Mountain Top Experiences?

Less than two months had passed since I received that prophetic word when I heard the voice of the Lord speak to my spirit man and say, "Move to Charlotte, North Carolina." I had only been to Charlotte twice before, both times related to ministry conventions, and hardly knew anyone there. My wife and I always have this thing that whenever we go to a city we have never been to before, we always rate our fondness for the city as to whether we could see ourselves living there. Back in 1995, we had an opportunity to visit Charlotte for the first time and both of us agreed we liked the "feel" of the city, never thinking that one day Charlotte would be our home. Now four years later the Lord spoke to me in 1999 and said, "Move to Charlotte."

Let me tell you just how wonderful the Lord is. At the job where I worked in New Orleans, they would post job vacancies for the company on the office bulletin board. Understand now, that I had developed a level of expertise in performing my job and the job tasks involved had become second nature to me. So, I was not actively looking for somewhere else to go. But on this particular day, I walked past the bulletin board and noticed a job vacancy in Apex, North Carolina. Well, I never heard of Apex and did not know its location related to Charlotte. But I knew I heard God say "Charlotte." So, I took the information down and called. The person I spoke with by telephone explained to me that Apex was the regional headquarters for the company, but the actual job position was located in Charlotte. I started laughing, recognizing that the Lord was up to something. I then called the office in Charlotte to get more information about the position. I found myself talking to the Regional Director, who just happened to be in the Charlotte office on that day. He just so happened to be at the office on that day interviewing applicants for the position. After talking for a while, he asked if I could come to Charlotte for an interview. I explained to him that I could not get away presently and he regretfully stated that he was looking to fill the position by the end of the week, which was three days away. We ended the conversation and I wished him well in his search. I remember telling the Lord, that if he wanted me in Charlotte, he would have to open up some doors that would allow me to provide financially for my family. Within a few minutes, the Regional Director called me back and asked if I would have a problem with interviewing over the telephone. I just about fell out of my chair when he asked that question. It was hard for me to conceal my joy at the opportunity to interview. We agreed and set up the interview for the following day. Everything went well and what was supposed to be a 15-minute interview turned into an hour-long conversation. Naturally, I felt pretty good about my chances of landing the job. After all, the Lord was in control of the situation, and I knew it. The Director called me back two days later and told me he had filled the position with a person who was already on staff and more familiar with the agency's operation, statewide contacts, and resources existing in North Carolina. I cannot begin to tell you how crushed I felt and begin to question whether God was playing tricks on me. Within 30 minutes after thanking the Director for the chance to interview and ending the phone call, he called me back stating he was so impressed by my interview that he created a brand-new position for me and asked if I would be willing to work for the company in Charlotte. I was making more money in my current job than I had ever made and decided I would not move my family for anything less than a specific amount. I told God that if relocating to Charlotte was his will for my family, my salary request would be met by this gentleman. After negotiating over what he could and could not offer by way of salary, the amount fell substantially short of what I had asked for. He explained that since this was a position he had just created, he was unsure how the position would be funded and where he would find the money to fund the position, let alone meet my salary request. I thanked him for the job offer but explained that it would not be in my best interest to uproot my family and move them so far from home. He understood and said he was sorry that we could not come to a mutual agreement. One day went by and I got another call from the Regional Director. He stated that he was able to switch some things around in his budget and had found a way to meet my salary request and asked how soon I would be able to start. Besides meeting my salary request, the company paid for my moving expenses to Charlotte and paid for my temporary housing in an upscale hotel in Charlotte for two months, while I worked on transitioning my family to North Carolina. In addition, they provided me with round-trip airline tickets to fly home and visit my family over the next two months. I initially moved to Charlotte in December of 1999 and after finding a permanent residence to live, moved my family in March of 2000. Once again, God was doing what he does best, and that is "Be God!" It appeared God was working overtime to make sure that what he had spoken to my spirit would come to pass. Although I thought I had settled in a place where I could finally move from tent to tabernacle, God said "NOT SO!" Instead, he disturbed my comfort zone, the place where I was, to the place of my "shall be." I had no better sense than to follow the cloud, realizing that the cloud was leading me to a place void of family, friends, or substantial connections. I felt a little like Abraham, leaving my home and kindred for a place that I knew not of. The one thing I did know was that wherever this place was, God had already prepared it just for me and my family.

CHAPTER 13

SCHOOL IS NOW IN SESSION

Things appeared to be coming in place in preparation for a deeper level of ministry. I was not sure where I was going, to be honest, but I sensed in my spirit that it was a better place for my family and me. But as always, before you can appreciate the freshness of tomorrow, there must be an inventory of yesterday. And so, I look back on past pastoral experiences not with disdain and disappointment, but rather with an appreciation for the life lessons I had learned. It was as if a class was in session, and I was seated at the desk of life's experiences.

Each step I took along the process of becoming was an opportunity to learn, grow, and develop. Most people come face to face with challenges and cease learning. I chose to use these challenges as stepping stones to a greater awareness of just who I was in God. Everything I went through in the name of ministry taught me a valuable lesson. Even as a former pastor, I learned pearls of wisdom that have since provoked me to a greater anointing in the spirit. Although both pastorates shared similarities, each was different in its ways. Both churches were located in rural areas of the states of Louisiana and Texas. Both churches were older, well-established churches but only had a handful of senior members. In each case, I started with less than a half-dozen members who were ingrained in their sedentary ways. Pastoring long distances, as each church was approximately 65-70 miles one way from my home, I was looked upon as a "city slicker" by various segments of the local community. Money was scarce, membership small, education limited, and vision lacking when I assumed the leadership of these churches. But one of the things that both churches had in common was the membership's genuine love for my family. Both churches had very small memberships but were mighty in their attitude and demonstration of love. The member's love could not be measured in dollars or cents or how much monetary compensation they could afford to seed into my life. But rather, their love was constantly on display as they sat receptively in church, eager to hear the Word of the Lord. The expressions on each of their faces, whenever my family would walk through the door, were evidence enough that purpose was being fulfilled. What I received from these and other members who became a part of our church family was a strong sense of loyalty, an undying commitment to be faithful, and a genuine desire to submit to the spiritual authority of their pastor. These people not only accepted me as their spiritual guide, but they also loved my children and wife. And for all the pastors reading this book, you know how difficult it can be when members love you but care little for your wife and children. Yes, I know I was positioned there to teach the people, but more times than I can remember, the people taught me. The experiences of serving those members taught me to appreciate "small things;" it taught me the value of serving others without notoriety or fanfare; it caused me to become sensitive to the needs of those less fortunate than myself; and it ushered me into an area where a desire was birthed in me to address the emotional, mental, relational, and spiritual lack in the lives of others.

I wish I could say that I did everything right. I wish I could tell you I was the greatest pastor in the world. I wish I could tell you that every member grew exponentially under my ministry. But if I told you that, both you and I would know that I was lying. It would be closer to the truth to tell you that I made more mistakes than I can count. I gave bad advice, I made poor decisions, and I listened to others when I should have been hearing from God. When it came to poor pastoring, you name it and I was probably guilty. But despite every mistake I made, I learned to "cover the sheep."

When it came to leading God's people, I did not have many mentors. Oh, I had many preachers who I admired and wanted to preach like, even mimicked at times. But there were not many pastors who I knew intimately and wanted to follow their examples of shepherding the flock of God. From where I stood, I saw evangelists trying their hand at pastoring, I saw pastors who should have remained singers, and I saw pastors in desperate need of training. Now mind you I am not condemning the pastors I observed, because I was pretty much in the same boat. But as I looked for a pattern to model myself after as a pastor, I came up short in identifying many such men.

Pastors that I saw and were esteemed as great leaders appeared to be more concerned with fame, fortune, and their future positioning than serving the people of God. I had a problem when the highlight of your year was the pastor's anniversary. To me, I thought the zenith of ministry would be the multitude of lives transformed by the saving power of Christ, the number of people miraculously healed of some incurable disease, or even the social and economic impact the ministry made on the surrounding community. But these events never seem to captivate the attention of the people or leader, as did the pastor's anniversary. In my experience, these were the times that churches pointed to for much of the year. I can recall one particular church that worked 6 months for the pastor's anniversary and the other 6 months for the church anniversary. When you completed one anniversary, you immediately started working towards the culmination of the other. So, it was in this environment that I looked at the pastors of my environment and wondered where I could find a mentor. I longed to be Elisha to someone's Elijah, Timothy to someone's Paul, or Joshua to someone's Moses.

Scripture tells us, "We have many teachers but not many fathers." I believe the first and greatest teacher in a child's life is his father. My father had been missing in my life since my birth. My biological father was never married to my mother and the first time I met him was when I was seventeen years old. So, there was always a void in my life for a father. Unbeknown to me at the time, I vicariously searched for a true father in the lives of ministers who crossed my path. I realize now that I placed an undue and sometimes overwhelming burden on the shoulders of some men. When they wilted under the pressure of fathership, I wrongfully laid the blame at their feet. As experience has taught me over time, many of those I tried to identify as mentors needed mentoring themselves. Some were not fathers, but merely sons acting like a father. But God placed a friend of mine in my life who, although only a few years older, Bishop Charles Brown mentored me even though he was not aware of the impact he had on my life. I came to admire this boy preacher when I was a child myself. This man would later perform the wedding ceremony between my wife and me several years later. Bishop Brown became my pattern in so many areas of my life. I learned about administration, dealing with people, setting the house in order, protocol, demonstrating a spirit of excellence and so many other things from this great man. This man took time out and invested in me. He made the kind of deposit in my life that I will be eternally grateful for. If not for his mentorship, counsel, wisdom, and love, I am unsure where my family and I would be today. He demonstrated a lifestyle of humility to me that to this day, I have yet to see in any other man. Although many took his humility as a sign of weakness, anyone who knows Bishop Brown knows he is a man of resounding courage, discipline, and determination. This man became more than a friend, pastor, and mentor; he became a father at a time when I needed affirming.

CHAPTER 14

A Recipe For Disaster

I received my first pastorate at the age of twenty-seven in Houma, Louisiana. I was living in New Orleans which was about sixty-five miles away. I remember being so excited about the opportunity to pastor. At the time I felt like I was ready for any and everything. Little did I know my apprenticeship in the ministry had not prepared me for the full scope of pastoring. I thought that being a pastor was an automatic step after Eldership. In school, the normal progression is to go from elementary to middle school, from middle to high school, and from high school to college. I thought being a pastor was the next step from being an Elder. But how many of you know that just because you are an Elder in the church, doesn't necessarily mean that you are a pastor at the next level? Being a pastor is a unique calling not everyone who is an Elder is destined to fulfill. Being a true pastor encompasses a life of self-denial and putting others' interests before your own and that of your family.

I had been sent by my superiors to a rural area of Louisiana and commissioned to "go and preach out the church." I didn't know it at the time, but I had been thrown to the wolves. The leadership of the church had cast me out into an ocean with a sink-or-swim mentality. Nothing I had endured in my ministry had prepared me for what I would encounter as a pastor. My Jurisdictional Bishop appointed me to the church, and I went in the "Spirit of the Lord." But what I soon discovered was that besides having the spirit of the Lord, I would have benefited tremendously if I also had training in administrative procedures, church politics, business and fiscal affairs, and the sound implementation of bringing a vision to fruition.

I had been sent out without any significant preparation. A vision had been cast by my leader, but no blueprint was provided to me on how to manifest it. They barked out orders "Forward March," but gave me no indication of the enemy I would encounter. They showed me a side of success but kept hidden the scars of defeat. So, I went, not knowing the direction to take. I fought, not knowing my enemy. I stood my ground, not understanding there are times when hiding is prudent.

Yes, they sent me in the name of the Lord, but where was the support system? Where was the undergirding infrastructure that is essential during the infancy stages of a new pastorate and ministry? Where was the financial backing that a young and struggling man, recently married with two small children needed to help offset ministry commitments? Where was it? Well, wherever it was, it wasn't at my disposal. What I came face to face with was the challenge of keeping the church's lights on, when lights at my own home were being disconnected. I had to keep the church's telephone on even if that meant my phone going silent. Because the church was the house of God and represented the physical place of his dwelling, I had to make sure that the church did not come under reproach. People were already saying that we would fail and couldn't make a difference in that rural area, and so I was determined not to fail. But I was fighting at a disadvantage. I was fighting with one hand tied behind my back, because despite all that I was doing, all that I knew how to do, it wasn't enough. It is like trying to repair a motor vehicle but not having the right tools to do the job. Oh, you may rig something up to get you to the next stop, but it becomes makeshift at best. You have a willingness to get the job done but lack the resources. I had the right attitude, but little aptitude on how to accomplish the goal. What I had on my hands was a recipe for disaster!

I believe every person who goes out to pastor a church needs to spend time under the watchful eye of a Senior Pastor, learning as an understudy and apprentice for the pastorate. Pastoral classes and training should be mandatory for the first-time pastor as well as refresher and evaluative tools made available for those shepherding a flock for the second or third time. It is vital to be able to assess what strengths the aspiring pastor possesses as well as what weaknesses may hinder or prevent him or her from completing their assignment. For those clergy taking up the task of shepherding again, this process becomes invaluable in identifying what things worked and were positive in the previous pastorate just as identifying what things were not successful and are not worth repeating the second time around. The assignment of a pastoral counselor could be made to assist the first-time pastor with pertinent decisions and issues that arise within the ministry. This person would not necessarily serve in an Assistant Pastor type role, but merely as a Wise Counselor to help offset the lack of experience and provide nurturing and guidance in delicate situations. This person would provide needed counsel and then have their role and presence slowly fade out over time. Ultimately, this person or someone like them would be a resource that the pastor would probably utilize over the life of his or her pastorate, even after their official assignment is long over.

CHAPTER 15

THE SCIENCE OF HOOP-A-LETICS

I always thought that if you could "hoop" you could preach. In fact, at one point in my ministry, I thought hooping was preaching. As far as I was concerned if a person didn't hoop, he didn't preach. "Hooping" for all of you who did not grow up in or matriculate from a Black church is another way of saying preaching. And not just any old preaching; but preaching your sermon in such a fervor that it stirs up people in an emotional frenzy. A lot of times it did not matter if you said anything of real substance or not, but as long as you could "tune up" you stood a pretty good chance of getting invited back to a particular venue. The ability to hoop became the hallmark of being known as a great preacher. You always wanted people leaving the church saying, "Man didn't he preach?" If people left your service in that frame of mind, then as a preacher you felt like you did your job.

But I have come to discover that what matters most in the proclaiming, is not the style but the substance. It is not so much in the method of delivery, evangelistic, expository, or the eloquence of your speech that matters. Rather it is more important that what you said impacted a person enough to cause them to make a decision to "change their life." If a person is affected enough to change something about themselves, be it their lifestyle, their commitment to God, or simply some bad habits, then the mission is accomplished. A professor of mine once told me the objective of preaching is to make the person "think." If you can get the person to stop long enough to think and reflect on his spiritual condition, then you have accomplished the purpose of ministry. It is The Word that convicts and brings those in need of repentance to the altar of sacrifice, not the oratorical skills of man.

I discovered in my maturation process that many facets go into making a great preacher, none of which has to do with how melodic or loud your voice may be. At the heart of every great preacher must be *passion*. What I'm referring to is the passion that was birth in the preacher long before he or she ever acknowledged God. For most of us, it was a passion that not only got us into trouble, but it has been passion unbridled, that has kept us in trouble. Samson had passion, David had passion, and Paul had passion. All the great leaders of our day had passion, something that drove them to do the things they did. Usually, that passion was after the flesh, and it caused them great pain. But isn't it strange that even after all these great men came to know God, he never did away with their passion? God knew that he could use these men despite their weaknesses. So instead of giving them a spiritual vasectomy, he changed the direction and control of their passion. Instead of being controlled by the flesh, they would now be led by the Spirit of God. God did not want to take the passion away from these men, for God gave them their passions, to begin with. But what he knew he had to do was change the object of their passion. So now instead of running after women, they would run after him. Instead of obeying man, they would obey him; and instead of fighting against the church, they would fight against the "world system." So, every anointed preacher needs passion.

Then that passion must be overshadowed by the inspiration that only comes from the Spirit of God. To touch the lives of people, you must be inspired by the Holy Ghost. The last time I checked, everyone has their own opinions and beliefs, everyone thinks their way is right, and all of us interpret things based on our past life experiences. But it is the Lord's breath, his *pneuma,* that engulfs the preacher and causes his Logos to become their Rhema. It is the revelatory Word of God that positions you in a place to uncover the mysteries of the Gospel; it forces you to take another look at yourself in the mirror that is God's Word. It is this Word that people are hungry for. For too long they have been placated with the words of Plato and Aristotle. Too long have they been made to listen to the oratorical skills of men. Whom they long to hear from is the Lord; "Is there a Word from the Lord?" They are tired of the same old warmed-over, leftover, and microwave messages that we have served up from our pulpits. We have given the people catchy slogans, sophisticated sayings, and hip-hop nursery rhymes, but no "fresh" Word. We have dazzled them with theatrical productions that we've called worship, but still no "anointed" Word. And it is the "Word" that the people need. Only the Word will satisfy the deep longing in their soul. Only the Word will fill the voided space in their lives. What people need today is a WORD that will usher in *True Deliverance*. I'm talking about the kind of deliverance that will remove the "taste" of sin from their mouth; the kind of deliverance that is everlasting. This kind of deliverance goes beyond a quick fix; it goes beyond a band-aid approach; it even goes beyond the need to come to the altar time and time again for the same issues. This kind of deliverance doesn't just mask the problem, it "destroys the yoke." This kind of deliverance cannot be found listening to someone else's tape; you won't discover it in a book; you can't even get it from second-hand testimonies; all of these are tools and methods that perhaps may supplement or complement the Word that God has placed in your spirit. But if you want to be an anointed preacher, the Spirit of God must birth that Word in YOU. Without God, your words become hollow echoes of man's wisdom. You become "sounding brass and tinkling cymbals." Your words will be proclaimed but it lacks the power to bring about true change. True change can only take place in the heart of man, which is the altar of God. The Lord declared, "No man comes to me except the father draws him." And inevitably, most people came to God because they "heard a Word." The Word may have come in the form of a song, a billboard, an announcement, or some other verbal message. But somehow the Lord was able to communicate with the person in the earth realm. "How can they hear without a preacher, and how can he preach except he be sent."

Finally, if a preacher is going to be a great preacher, then he should possess a genuine love for people. There should be a positive relationship between priests and people. This may sound a little crazy because so many times we hear preachers that we do not know and have no relationship with. The Bible tells us to "know them that labor among us." So how can we have relationships with preachers whom we do not know or who are just passing through? You know them by the Spirit of God. How many times have you sat and listened to a preacher who had been hyped up to be an outstanding minister, only to discover through the Spirit that something was not quite right? The Bible warned us to "try the spirit by the Spirit." In this way, we keep ourselves clear of false teachers and preachers. We live in a day now where preachers and ministries are marketed just like automobiles. They are presented with all the "bells and whistles" that the media has to offer. Just because you are on television five times a week does not correlate with the level of anointing you may have. What you may have is a good business mind, and a good bankroll supporting your ministry. But the person who has not made it to television and is traveling by car across the country, preaching in small-town America, may have an anointing that dwarfs the televangelist. But because we do not get a chance to see him unless we attend his meetings, we may be left with the impression that what is presented before our eyes is true ministry. And if we make that assumption based on the number of times one appears on television or based on the amount of media coverage one commands, or the amount of money one raises in church meetings, then we will always miss the boat as to the real move of God.

CHAPTER 16

Discovering Worship

When I arrived in Charlotte, North Carolina, I had the attitude that I pretty much knew all there was to know about the church. It was not that I thought I knew everything or was some kind of expert but having grown up in the church all my life, I didn't think there were too many things I had not been exposed to or did not know. Boy, was I mistaken!

Coming to Charlotte meant moving in the natural but, as I later discovered, it provoked a move in the Spirit also. I had grown up amid praise. Praise was what I had become accustomed to. Even though it is a rare site to see me dance before the Lord now, I can recall the time when I would dance and shout till times got better. I remember times when I danced so until I danced right out of my shoes and shirt. In our church, you really did not have church unless you had a good shout. Long before Kirk Franklin came out with the song "Stomp," we were used to "picking them up and putting them down." I mean I was in churches where people were doing moves that would leave James Brown, Michael Jackson, and Usher scratching their heads. So, when the song "Praise Is What I Do" came out, I had already been doing that for thirty-five years. But God was taking me to another place that I never knew about in the spirit. It was the place of worship.

I found a place called worship that I did not know previously existed. I used to think that if praise could not do it, you did not need it. But I came to discover that praise is the precursor to worship. It is almost like the foreplay in the chambers of a husband and wife that leads to the ultimate moment of intimacy. The foreplay is nice and enjoyable, but it is not until the actual act of consummation that you become one with the other. All of us back then knew how to praise, but few of us had ever learned what it meant to worship. In my spiritual immaturity and ignorance, I thought what black people did in the church was praise and what white people did was worship. I recall times when we would mock and make fun of those in white churches with their hands lifted, off-beat clapping, and laying prostrate on the floor. We would not be caught dead imitating our white counterparts. For us, the movements had to be more spectacular. For many of us, it became more of a show, more of an exercise in bodily activity than about reciprocating the affection of the lover of your soul.

I was always caught up in the "God bless me" attitude. But as I continued to mature in the spirit it birthed in me a desire to "bless the Lord." My introduction to Life Center Ministries allowed me to be introduced to people like, then Pastor, and later, Bishop Brian Moore, Pastors Tammy Renee Glenn, and Lamar Simmons, some of God's greatest worshippers. God, through these vessels, taught me about worship in ways that I had never known. When I joined The Life Center of Charlotte ministry, Pastor Moore had the members engaged in reading a book entitled, "God Chasers" by Tom Tienny. After reading that book, my life changed, and was launched on a different trajectory regarding worship. I had been thinking I "knew" the Lord intimately, only to discover he was still behind the veil. When I had finished reading the book, I began to weep like a baby. For at that moment, I realized I had been seeking God's hand and not his face. "God Chasers" provoked me to go after the face of God, to feel his breath upon my face and hear him whisper in my ear; yes, this is the place where I longed to be, wanted to be, needed to be, and had to be.

All of those years I thought I was a worshipper, but I found out, I was one of those lingering in the outer courts. The true essence of worship cannot be found in the outer courts. You recall the Sanctuary Solomon built with its' outer court, inner court, and Holy of Holies. Outside of the outer court, there was the Profane Place and the Most Outer Court. People in these areas of the sanctuary had no desire to be found in the place of worship. The outer court was the place where everyone gathered. It was the most popular place for here you found the butcher, the baker the candlestick maker. This is the place where people came to network; they came to impress each other with their outlandish testimonies; they came to the outer court to "spectate." In the outer court, you became accustomed to feeling comfortable, for it was the place of least resistance and greatest conformity. Here everyone looked alike, acted alike, and talked alike. The outer court was a good place to be if you wanted to make friends. Here you could get away with doing the same old thing. Here everyone was busy duplicating and imitating each other. In the outer courts, people spend time contemplating being another Benny Hinn, Pastor John Hannah, or Pastor Cheryl Brady. Change here is defined by promise, not manifestation; change here is measured by degrees, not complete turnarounds; and in the outer court, you are evaluated by who you are, not what you are becoming. Yes, this is the place of "arrival" where the church has learned to be contented. As long as you were in the outer courts everyone recognized your "outward display" of worship. Here you could fool others into believing that you were a worshipper because you imitated the things that worshippers did. You knew the right things to say, you knew how to wave your hand just right, you knew how to speak in tongues, you knew when to lift your voice and when to dance. You had excelled in the art of the chameleon. Being able to adapt, camouflage, and blend in with any atmosphere became second nature for some. But how many of you know that God is calling you past the outer court and into the inner court?

The inner court is smaller in size and scope because fewer people are willing to pay the price or make the necessary sacrifices to leave the outer court. Here in the inner court, the limelight is dimmer, the audience smaller, the sacrifice greater, and the price costlier. To get to the inner court you must leave certain relationships behind. Many of these relationships are the same ones that you took an enormous amount of time to cultivate, to get them just where you wanted them to be. You invested time, money, blood, sweat, and tears into certain people and waited for your investment to pay dividends. But if you are serious about getting closer to God, your moving into the inner court will cause you to "kiss" your investment goodbye. You come to understand that what you thought was an investment to bring you benefits, really was an investment to usher you into your place of destiny. You recognized that the relationships were nice while they lasted, but there comes a point where you have got to move on. The relationship was good then, but it cannot help me now. It was for a season, but as you know seasons come and seasons go. If you allow yourself to remain attached to relationships past their season, the same relationships that were a blessing before now become a curse. The Apostle Paul acknowledged his "shifting season" when he said, "When I was a child I spoke as a child, but when I became a man, I put away childish things." When you understand and are willing to go to another place in God, it does not matter what or who you may have to give up. But understanding moving into the inner court will produce change. It will also cost you something dear to your heart. Did you ever stop and recognize that God never asks for our hand-me-downs or the leftovers we are willing to part with? God always asks us for our most prized possessions to test our love for him.

Remember Abraham? God knew Abraham loved him and he could have asked for a sacrifice that Abraham would have quickly and easily offered up. But instead, he demanded Abraham's son, his only begotten son, and the son of promise. Abraham took two young lads with him up into the mountain when he went to offer Isaac up as a burnt offering. But when he got to a certain point, he told the young men to wait there while he and Isaac went further to worship. He understood that the closer he got to God, the more things and people had to leave by the wayside. He could not take everyone with him into his place of destiny. Finally, as he and Isaac trudged up the mountainside, his son looked curiously at him and said, "We have the wood, we have the fire and knife, but where is the sacrifice?" If we are going to experience true worship, God will require something to die. And it is not until we pass the test of being able to offer up our most prized and beloved possessions to the Lord, that we are ready to enter the Holy of Holies.

The Holy of Holies was the place where the High Priest entered once a year to offer up sacrifices for the people. This was the "Most Holy Place" where the very presence of God dwelt. No man, not even the High Priest could enter this most sacred place defiled or unworthy. Before entering the Most Holy Place the priest would stop by the Laver where he washed his hands. The Laver was a basin made from the mirrors of the women where the priest would wash his hands. He could not wash his hands without seeing a reflection of himself. That is one of the things true worship does. Worship provokes you to see yourself in the presence of God. He would also tie a belt around his waist and wear bells on the hem of his garment before stepping beyond the inner veil. The bells were a signal to the people that the priest was still alive. If the priest were to enter the Holy of Holies without being pure, he would die right there on the spot. And because no man could go into the Holy of Holies, the priest would have to be literally pulled out by the rope.

Imagine what today would be like if God would start killing those of us who enter into his presence unfit. The Most Holy Place is not a place for the timid of heart for here is where God is. It is the place where we have confronted our demons, been victorious, and are now ready to see God "face to face." This is the place where we have become transparent to the Father and have unclothed our humanity before him. It is funny how even though God looks at the heart of man and sees past our facades, we dress up and pretend that God is blind and cannot see beyond our presentation. But the truth of the matter is that despite God's omniscience, he is waiting for us to enter the chamber and involuntarily undress before him. This exposes our vulnerability to the Father and acknowledges to him that we are indeed his and his alone. It is here in this most sacred place that God shows himself to us in the purest form that our flesh will allow us to contain. For we know that no man can see God face-to-face and live. Our mortal bodies cannot contain the glory that is the brightness of his expression.

Here in the Holy of Holies, we have long ceased to desire to be another Cindy Trimm, Creflo Dollar, or Rod Parsley. We are now open to God creating who HE wants us to be. We understand in this place that personalities are finite, limited, and relative. Before Dr. Bill Winston there was an Oral Roberts; before Oral Roberts, there was a Billy Graham; before Billy Graham, there was a Charles Harrison Mason; before Charles Harrison Mason there was a William Seymour. Each of these personalities were used by God in their time and for a season. Here in the Holy of Holies, we understand that if any of these came on the scene before or after their time, they would not have been as effective as they have been. So, when you get to the Holy of Holies your prayer must not be "Lord make me another Bishop Alfred Owens, Bishop Brian Moore, or Dr. Joyce Meyer. Instead, our prayer must reflect our Savior's prayer in the garden when he said, "not my will, but thine be done." For in this place, I cease to be concerned with the noise from the outer court. Here I have moved past the sacrifices of getting into the inner court. Now I am prepared for the "process" of the Holy of Holies. Here is where I'm staying until God does what he wants to do with his vessel. It is a process that will now shift me to another place in God, another dimension, another Paradigm. I have moved past the "Profane Place" to the Most Outer Court; from the Most Outer Court to the Outer Court; from the Outer Court to the Inner Court; from the Inner Court past the Laver, past the outer veil, and stepped into the Holy of Holies. Thank God the bells are still ringing! I hear the bells of the priest. Ring-a-ling, ring-a-ling! Can you not hear the bells? They are ringing, the alarm is sounding, and the clarion call is still being answered. I am now ready because I found this new place called worship.

CHAPTER 17

Shifting To A New Paradigm

As I moved in the natural from New Orleans to Houston, back to New Orleans, and then to Charlotte, I found myself gradually shifting from church ministry to Kingdom ministry. Each physical relocation coincided with relocation in the Spirit. I was unaware that what was occurring with me in the natural was a mirrored reflection of what was taking place in the Heavenlies. Changing locations, being promoted to higher paying jobs, more work responsibilities and the growth of my family had a direct correlation to what was going on in the Spirit. The shifting to a new paradigm was taking place.

Church ministry was what I had known and been doing my entire life. It had come to the point that I was doing the work of the Lord, but over time had become distanced from the Lord of the Work. I was still preaching and teaching, working and counseling, singing and shouting, raising offerings, and being a blessing people. But the place where God was taking me now, Kingdom Ministry, had more to do with speaking a Rhema Word in season, being found in the posture of worship, raising people and not money, and sowing seed instead of giving money. I once saw the lines of Church and Kingdom and they were very much intertwined. As the shifting in my spirit continued to manifest, I came to be able to differentiate between the two and my focus became clearer. This may not mean anything to you but for me, this was my "coming of age," from spiritual childhood to manhood. Moving from church to a Kingdom mentality was like being reborn all over again. This maturation process introduced me to a concept I had not experienced before. Up until this point, the word Kingdom was just a catchy new phrase. It was the new flavor of the month. Everyone was saying it and I think most people, including myself, had no idea what it entailed.

Church had me focused on my position with men. Shifting to the mindset of Kingdom, I became more concerned with my position with God. In church, pleasing man was the top priority. The kingdom is all about pleasing God. In church, I ran after the counsel of men. Kingdom taught me to seek the wisdom of God. At church, I was consumed with meeting the needs of everyone else. Kingdom began to teach me about walking in the purpose that God had for me. In church, I accepted all engagements, and in Kingdom, I learned to ask the Lord for his approval before saying yes to any assignments. In church, I became frustrated by the deeds of others because my focus was on "man." Kingdom began to teach me the deeds of men were only a distraction keeping me from reaching my destiny in God. In church the voice of others was predominant. In Kingdom, I now listen to hear the voice of God. In church, my goal was to become connected to the "right people." Kingdom taught me to pursue and get connected to God. In church, I thought I had reached perfection when "all men" spoke well of me.

Kingdom told me, "Woe to you when all men speak well of you." So, I stopped trying to conceal my imperfections before people and allowed myself to be transparent with the one who knew me best, my Lord and Savior, the only perfect man, Jesus the Christ!

It was the realization that "the perfect man" was not someone who never committed a sin or fell, but rather it was one who, as Donnie McClurkin recorded, "we fall down but we get up." I now understood the perfect man was someone who had become mature and "seasoned" in the Lord. Mature to the extent that things that previously had been a struggle and a source of bondage no longer held the power of captivity. It was like the things that caused me to hurt and cry yesterday would no longer have the same devastating effect on me. I was in the process of transitioning from spiritual childhood to spiritual manhood. It is as Paul declared in Hebrews 6:1, "leaving the principles of the doctrine of Christ, let us go on to perfection." This lets me know that each time you face a spiritual challenge and overcome it, you are now eligible to be promoted to a higher level in Christ.

I know we have heard it said time and time again, "With every new level, comes a new devil." That is not just a slogan. In the natural, there is a systematic progression of life. I have never seen a newborn baby start out walking from birth. Ultimately the baby will walk provided the absence of medical or physical abnormalities. But there is a progressive process that occurs before walking takes place. First, the baby learns to hold its head up. Soon the baby begins to crawl. After learning how to prompt himself up by pulling up on a table or other object, he gets to the point where he takes a step or two and inevitably falls. This falling and getting back up is repeated until the baby begins to walk without assistance. With each level of transition comes an equal level of challenge. You may say that since the goal is for the baby to walk, would it be better and less painful for the child to be able to move from the crib to walking? If that were to happen just imagine all of the wonderful things that baby and his parents would miss out on. For instance, not being able to walk causes the parent to have to pick up and hold the baby and carry or transport him whenever needed. This creates a special bonding where the power of a touch, cuddling, and bonding occurs. As the baby's body continues to develop his leg muscles begin to strengthen because of him pulling himself up by holding onto objects such as a table. Soon he can support his own weight. All during this time, he is building and developing the characteristics of resilience and persistence as he repeatedly picks himself up time after time and tries again. He continues to learn how to build trust in adults as his parents are a few feet from him motioning him to "come to mama, come to daddy." His self-confidence grows exponentially as he is challenged by those who continually encourage him to take a step by saying, "You can do it." As a result of this process, these children will find themselves taking their first steps anywhere between 9 and 12 months and walking by the time they are 14 or 15 months old. You now understand the beauty and benefits of having this child navigate this process…which does not happen overnight.

Just as the baby is not successful on his first few attempts, so it is with us. We are not made perfect overnight. Becoming who God has ordained us to be takes time. Although God sees us as we shall be, we see ourselves in the "process of becoming." God lives in eternity and what shall be, already is. But to us who are governed by Chronos time, we only see the beginning and by faith, the end. It is the journey between the start and finish that God in his sovereign will, keeps hidden from us. God speaks to Abram in Genesis 12:2 and tells him "I will make of thee a great nation." But he does not reveal to Abram what he will go through before he becomes a great nation. Nor does he tell Abram he will be asked to offer his son of promise as a burnt offering.

By walking in divine purpose toward our God-ordained destinies, we discover an untapped source of strength that we never knew was there before. As we continue to move forward, we come to the knowledge that "we can do all things through Christ" who strengthens us. Yes, it is Christ that strengthens but it is in "us," that he places his divine power. So when challenging situations arise in your life and you seek the strength of others (your pastor, your mother or relative, or your covenant partner), and they are nowhere to be found, it is not for you to give up hope and wave the white flag of surrender; but rather to look deep in the recesses of your spirit man and declare that "I am more than a conqueror," or "no weapon formed against me," or "I will let nothing separate me from the love of God." I and me, though small words, are not necessarily indicative of the stature of an individual. Some will think little of themselves and the power that is God and act accordingly. Do not be like the 10 Israelite spies in Numbers 13:33 who were sent to spy out the "Promised Land" and brought back a report of what they saw to Moses. They did as Moses commanded and went and spied out the land, its inhabitants, and the land's fruitfulness. In their report back to Moses and the children of Israel they confirmed that the land was fruitful but added, "We saw giants in the land, and we were in our own sight as grasshoppers and so we were in their sight." Too often we see our obstacles as giants and ourselves as mere grasshoppers, helpless to do anything. I have learned that one of Satan's chief tricks is to get us to magnify the problem instead of the "Answer." I can recall years ago singer Andre Crouch singing, "Jesus is the Answer for the world today, above him there's no other Jesus is the Way." We give up thinking that there is no way we can overcome the obstacle in front of us. But for those of us who recognize that we serve a Great Big God, who has placed HIS TREASURE in our earthen vessels, we have come to embrace Proverbs 23:7 which states, as a man "thinketh in his heart, so is he." Ultimately, we become what we can envision or think of ourselves. Jesse Jackson says it this way, "If my mind can conceive it and my heart believe it, I know I can achieve it." If your mind can grasp this truth, you can begin to walk in your true God-ordained purpose.

CHAPTER 18

Anointed For Purpose

I have come to understand divine destiny as I never had before. Today we are inundated with words such as purpose and destiny. Almost every preacher, religious television program, or song, mentions these concepts if not directly, then by implication. I believe the church world has gotten caught up with this fad just like it did when everyone was spouting the prayer of Jabez, "Enlarge my territory." The church has used the words destiny and purpose so much, like me, I am not sure they fully grasp the significance of their meaning. We used these words to inform someone that we were headed somewhere. But based on our 360-degree personal theology we have no idea where that place exists. It sounds spiritual and "deep" when we mention the words, "purpose and destiny," but I contend much of the church is merely "marking time" and living at the surface level of our potential in God. It is as if we are standing on the walking conveyor belt that we see at airports or escalators in shopping malls. The conveyor belt is designed to propel us forward without having to make manual steps ourselves. I recall many times walking "against the flow" of the movement of the belt. No matter how much I walked the opposite way, I somehow never managed to reach my starting place. So, it is with many of us. Instead of moving "with" the flow of the Spirit, too often we find ourselves going against the grain only to find ourselves many years later in nearly the same place. Think about it. How long have some of our churches been collecting for their building fund? Please let me know when you see a new edifice or major repairs completed. How many years have we been attending bible study? Yet we can only quote St. John 3:16 and still have trouble with Psalm 23. Remember Moses and the children of Israel? They kept moving for 40 years in the desert. The problem was they were moving but going nowhere. God finally told them in Deuteronomy 2:3, "You've walked around this mountain long enough. Turn northward." They were moving but going around in circles. So, what appears for some to be a progression toward destiny, in reality, is a "camouflaged status quo." And it is in the false security of this camouflaged state where the real danger lies.

God's marching order for us is "forward march!" Yes, there are times when God will have us "stand still," but in those moments, it is to witness the supernatural manifestation of the power of God. God is a proceeding, progressing, and continuing God. Our God never resides in retreat. He deals with addition and multiplication. Even in his subtraction, he finds a way to add. He reduced Gideon's army in Judges, chapter 7, from 32,000 down to 300 soldiers. He wanted to prove to the Israelites that true power belonged to God and not man. There are times when people truly believe they are walking in their purpose when in fact they have no idea of what God's purpose is for their lives.

How do we discover God's purpose for our lives? Who told us what his purpose was for our lives? Was it the Bishop? What about our Pastor? No, maybe it was our dear beloved mother, or maybe our prayer partner. Maybe we discover our purpose by reading a book or receiving a "sign?" Surely if we attend a prophetic conference and are fortunate to be called out and get a "word" spoken into our lives, who better to know our purpose than the prophet? Not dismissing the anointing of God upon the ministering gifts named above, but could it be that we are too busy hearing from everyone else that we missed hearing from God? We missed God so badly at times the voice that we thought was his, belonged to an embodied voice of error. No matter how well-intentioned they might have been, when men choose to speak over the lives of others they inevitably, and at times, error! Notice I said when men choose to speak for God. This is when the spirit of error enters our flesh and causes us to "miss" God. But if we learn how to become sensitive to God's voice and allow HIM to speak to us, we will come to know what his will is for our lives. To become familiar with his voice we must develop a relationship with the Father. Only then will we be able to discern our Lord's voice and know it is HE who is calling us to our destined place.

I am convinced that many people are focused on what they believe to be their destiny without understanding their purpose. It is like knowing the ending of a novel or movie without knowing the challenges the main character had to go through to get to the end. The apostle John in the book of Revelation saw a great multitude of people dressed in white robes but did not know who they were. One of the 24 elders informed John, "These are they which came out of great tribulation and have washed their robes, and made them white in the blood of the Lamb." God thought it important enough that he took the time to testify about the struggles they overcame in fulfilling their purpose. He wanted John to know these fulfilled their purpose before achieving their destiny. Scripture reveals that we were foreordained in Christ before the very foundation of the world. The divine purpose must emanate from a Divine source. Man is not the divine source. Books are not the divine source. Philosophies are not the divine source. Religious denominations are not the divine source. There is only one Divine source, and that source is the true and living God. Everything else serves as a complimentary resource. The Lord declared that when he said, "Heaven and earth shall pass away but my words shall not pass away."

When you walk in purpose you walk in the Spirit of the Lord to accomplish whatsoever, HE desires. Galatians 5:16 states, "Walk in the spirit, and you shall not fulfill the lust of the flesh." Walking in the Spirit is the only way to know that you are walking in your purpose. For the Spirit of God will "lead and guide you into all truths." The Spirit of God then becomes the teacher, the Paraclete that guides your yielded spirit through its journey. On this journey, you will face obstacles, detours, and roadblocks. If you are submitted to him and commit to doing it God's way, then he will lead and guide you. God's Word will become a "light unto your path and a lamp unto your feet." It literally will illuminate the dark places along your path and allow you to avoid destruction. The Bible says in Psalm 37:23, "The steps of a good man are ordered by the Lord." The Word of God will help you to overcome every stumbling block, every pitfall, every pothole, and every dead end along your path. God's word will cause you to end up in a safe, secure, and mature place in him. Notice I did not say a more convenient or feel-good place in God. If the truth be told many of the places we find ourselves are places we would rather not be. Many of the things we endured along our journey, if left up to us we would have bypassed altogether and taken a shortcut. Could that be why the Lord often reveals the beginning and the end but hides the middle from us? Remember Abraham? God called him and told him to "go," and I will make you a "father of many nations." Sounds like the beginning and the end. But if he had revealed what it would take for him to have to go through to become the father of many nations, I am not so sure Abraham would have accepted the assignment. Know that fulfilling God's purpose comes with a price.

A friend of mine once preached a sermon entitled, "The Anointing Costs." Many of us are seeking a blue light special, a markdown bargain, or a clearance price when it comes to the anointing. We seek to find a way to obtain the anointing without paying FULL PRICE. "Salvation is FREE, but the anointing costs." Many of us long to be in God's presence. But are you willing to pay the costs? For every item that has worth, the manufacturer attaches a price of comparable value. When you contemplated purchasing that special item in the store you immediately took inventory of your resources as part of your decision to purchase the item. Based on your assessment you either purchased the item, placed it on lay-away, passed on buying it at all, or decided now was not the time to invest. Some purchased the item with cash because they had the resources at hand. Others purchased the item on credit planning to buy it over time. Some decided the cost was too much to pay and left the item there. Finally, some understood they did not have the necessary funds at the time and placed the item on what we have come to know as "layaway." These folks recognized that they were not able or ready to pay the full price of the item at that moment. However, they wanted it known that "this is mine" and placed a "down payment" to hold the item to return and claim full ownership once they had gathered what was needed. I admire this kind of person because they will step out on faith and make an initial investment, not fully knowing how or when they will be able to afford the item. Can someone shout "FAITH!" The prophet Habakkuk and Apostle Paul declared in scripture that "the just shall live by faith." If God were to give you his anointing without you paying full price for it, then he would be no more than a hustler, a scam artist, or a vendor looking to make a deal. God is not in the business of clearance sales, markdowns, or discount deals. You and I did not choose God, rather he chose us. And if we are going to enter covenant with him, St. Matthew 22:37 gives us the criteria, which is "love the

Lord with all thy heart, and with all thy soul, and with all thy mind." It will always be "God's Way or No Way." We love bargains and are always looking for the best deal. In the grand scheme of God's will, however, there are no shortcuts to fulfilling our purpose. If it means wandering in your wilderness for 40 years until all the dead weight falls off, so be it. If you must go into a fiery furnace of affliction to purify your character, he will allow it to be. The Lord will not barter, compromise, or bargain with anyone when it comes to releasing his anointing. You can receive the anointing if you really want it but understand it will cost you everything!

CHAPTER 19

Where Healing Begins

In the weeks before moving from New Orleans to Charlotte, the Lord spoke to me and told me to move to Charlotte. My wife is a woman of faith, and she has been my inspiration for many years. I moved to Charlotte in December of 1999 and left my family in New Orleans while I looked for a residence for us to reside. When I would call back home, she would ask, "have you heard from God yet?" And every day it became harder to tell her, "Not a word yet." Over the next three months, I lived in a hotel and later found a small apartment. Having to tell my wife the same thing every day got to the point where I told her, "God must have gone on strike because he stopped talking to me after moving to Charlotte." I became frustrated with God and said to him, "now that you have me here, why Charlotte?" I found myself praying, fasting, and going on consecrations seeking God for an answer. Three months after my initial move to Charlotte from Louisiana, I transitioned my wife and children to Charlotte in March 2000. God had gone silent on me and left me without a "proceeding word."

My family and I began attending Pastor John P. Kee's ministry, New Life Fellowship. The ministry's motto was "The Place Where Healing Begins." As I sat under Pastor Kee's teaching, I began to recall the words of this young man who stood outside of my home in Slidell, Louisiana, telling me I needed healing. New Life became another place of transition, but one where my healing would begin. Pastor Kee has a ministry unlike any I had seen before. New Life ministered to the hurting, undervalued, and unchurched in a way I had never seen. I saw sisters with nose piercings and brothers looking like pimps sitting in the front rows as if they were church mothers and deacons. Pastor Kee and New Life hosted a weekend activity entitled the "Praise Connection." Disco balls were hanging from the ceiling, a dance floor, hostesses serving food, and people having a ball. If you did not know any better, you would have thought you stepped into a nightclub instead of a church. I thought, "Here is a pastor who is not afraid to reach out to what the church world labeled, the "dregs" of society. Not only did he reach out to them, but he also adopted them and made them a part of his church family." Instead of calling them members, everyone was known as a "Partaker." I had been in many churches where people such as these had been invited to come and worship. But few ever came for fear of being judged, condemned, and treated as second-class humans. The beauty of New Life's environment lies in having doctors and college professors sitting next to drug addicts and prostitutes. The person sitting there with the nose ring and tattoo could have easily been the college professor as opposed to the drug addict. Despite how each person dressed or looked everyone was welcomed and treated with respect and dignity and shown the love of Christ.

New Life Fellowship was the place where healing began, not only for my wife and me, but also for my three wonderful children who were 16, 15, and 11 years old at the time. We had known Pastor Kee for almost five years by this time, and he was somewhat familiar with our background. He knew I had pastored before. I was concerned he would attempt to get us involved in the church's activities, and neither my wife nor I were ready for that. Instead, he discerned we were in a place where we needed healing and allowed us to "be still" as he ministered to us like every other partaker. I know from experience now that one of the worst things a pastor can do is rush a new member into ministry work because of their gifting or ability. As a pastor or leader, it is vital that you allow time for the new member to acclimate themselves to their new environment and allow them to "sit" for a while.

At New Life, the Lord continued to expose me to an element in the church I was not familiar with. I call these people, "the overlooked." These are the people I believe Jesus would be hanging out with today if he were walking the earth. But these are not the people we see in most of our churches on Sunday mornings. Most of the people we encounter on Sunday morning are dressed appropriately, have good hygiene, and have no problems "talking to our neighbors." But these are the same members that inflict the greatest hurts and cause the deepest wounds. Yes, they drive the best cars, wear designer clothes, give the largest offerings, and are usually very demonstrative when it comes to praising

God. These are the same ones who sing your praises on Sunday and gossip about you on Monday. These are the ones who expose your worst to show their best. These are the ones who count you out, assassinate your character, rejoice over your failures, minimize your successes, and attempt to keep you isolated from others who possess a caring heart.

But these were not the kind of people we encountered at New Life Fellowship. At New Life, we met many persons struggling to make ends meet, but gladly shared what they had with you. Here you felt like one of the family. I came to understand why Pastor Kee called his parishioners, Partakers. We were all partakers because we had all things in common, a joint inheritance with Christ. This mentality permeated the entire ministry and allowed people who came right off the streets in their hand-me-down clothes to feel just as important as preachers and mothers in their Sunday best. It was during the time, 1990-1997 we lived in Houston, Texas that my spiritual transformation began, and the layers of religion started to peel away from my eyes. It was here in Charlotte, North Carolina however where the light bulb moment and my spiritual "rebirthing" manifested in full. Before relocating to Charlotte, positions, people, and titles had become so ingrained in my mindset that I failed to see God had people that I had overlooked. Here I began to see people who had no titles, no positions, but had the favor of God. Was I any better than the addict sitting beside me? Was I more deserving of God's love than the ex-con sitting on the next row? I discovered if it had not been for the grace of God, I could have turned out another way. I came to realize it was God's mercy that hid me and kept me from being exposed like so many others. God kept my mess covered and gave me time to get it right. Praise God!

So here I sat, bruised, and hurt, but healing fast. I was wounded, broken, and scarred but the healing process had already begun. There are times we trust God in one particular area of our lives, but not the other. We may believe God for a new car or a promotion on our job but dare not trust him to heal a broken relationship or an incurable disease. It is by one Spirit that God operates. He does not have one spirit in charge of material things and another with relationships and still another with physical healings. Ephesians 4:4 gives us to know that it is by "one Spirit" that we all are called. Indeed, it was the Spirit of the Lord that led us to New Life where my family and I discovered a place where healing could begin. As our healing began to manifest itself, the Lord began shifting us again. We were just becoming settled here and I was looking forward to working in ministry when the Lord "impressed upon me" it was time to go to work, but it would not be at New Life. Our family received the strength and love from Pastor Kee and New Life Fellowship to go further. Like Abraham, we left not knowing where we were going. Over the next six months, we visited several ministries, none of which the Lord led us to connect with. It was not that there were no anointed ministries in the city, for there were tremendous men and women of God who were leading dynamic ministries. Once again, the

Lord had us in a holding pattern. I finally told my wife that if we did not find a church home soon, we may have to consider returning home to New Orleans. In the back of my mind, I began to wonder if God moved us to heal us. I reasoned within myself maybe Charlotte was just the place of our separation and healing. We continued to seek the Lord in prayer for guidance.

Two weeks later my wife told me about a preacher that had recently started a ministry in Charlotte, North Carolina and she was going to attend his service. By now my wounds were healed from people, but I found myself less excited about church. No matter how anointed you consider yourself to be, if you stay "unconnected" with the people of God long enough you will find the enthusiasm that once was vibrant, slowly fading away. After visiting this ministry Elleanor returned home all excited. She said to me, "you have to come and hear this preacher." After her second visit, I gave in and accompanied her to the service.

The ministry was holding its church services at the Hilton Hotel on W.T. Harris Boulevard in Charlotte. Even after hearing my wife rave about the preacher, I was skeptical about going. Although the ministry was non-denominational, the pastor had come out of the African Methodist Episcopal Zion Church reformation. I had already made up in my mind there was nothing an AME Zion preacher could teach me. You know God was setting me up right? It was June 3, 2001, and I went to the Sunday morning service and purposely sat in the rear of the room. I wanted to make sure I had the perfect view to check out everything that went on in service. I watched how people acted. I took note of how people were greeted at the door and escorted to their seats. I noted how orderly the children behaved, how the offering was facilitated, and how well the musicians played. I mean I watched everything!

It was time for the message and on this Sunday, there was a guest pastor from Tallahassee, Florida. I was blessed to hear a dynamic message from another young pastor, but I had not come to hear him. I thought to myself, "okay you came, and the pastor you came to hear, did not preach." So, I felt like it was a blank trip. During announcements, it was announced that the pastor would be speaking at a church service that coming Thursday in a nearby city. My wife and I agreed to go and hear him. After arriving at the church, we were ushered halfway towards the front and had very good seats. It was a very large Baptist church, and the place was jammed packed. It was time for the Word and Pastor Brian Moore was introduced. His message for the evening was entitled "One Last Cry." By the time he finished preaching, I looked around and what I observed was an entire church in chaos and pandemonium. Some people were crying, some running, some worshipping and some laid prostrate on the floor, but everyone had been profoundly touched.

Over the previous years, I have been blessed to hear some of Christendom's most anointed preachers. But I had never heard a man preach like this man. Indeed,

I had been blessed to hear many great preachers and speakers, but there was something uniquely different about this man. Pastor Moore ministered a Word that night which resuscitated Life back into my spirit man. It was as if someone literally applied defibrillators to my chest and jump-started my heart back to beating again. There was a fresh and liberating "sound" about the Word he ministered that I had missed for a long time. Yes, I had heard other preachers who had the Word of God in their mouths. Yes, they were also anointed, gifted, knowledgeable, and spirited. But something was extremely different about this man. A lot of preachers speak about their own life, but this man did not merely speak about his life, he spoke "from his life." There is a difference. Many of us talk about our lives as if we have somehow managed to become disconnected from whatever it was that made us who we are. But now and then a person can speak from his own life and takes you to a place where it seems he is still in the midst of his struggles. "One Last Cry" was not only his plea to the Lord, but he stepped over pews and rows of seats to make each one of the persons in the audience identify right along with him. I felt as if Jesus was passing by, and I had one last opportunity to get his attention. Would I allow the religious environment to stifle my call to the Lord? Here I was, third generation COGIC, sitting in a Baptist church listening to a former AME Zion preacher. I felt that if a difference was going to be made in my life, I had one last opportunity to get God's attention. I had one last cry left in me and no devil in hell or the church was going to stop me. I was determined that no one, no situation, and no circumstance would interrupt my worship. I was determined that I would do whatever was necessary to arrest God's attention as he passed by. Yell, scream, call out, jump, lay prostrate, cry, run, whatever it took to get his attention, in that moment I was determined to connect back with my Father. It became clear to me that I did not need a title, a position, praise of man, or a pat on the back. What I needed was God! I needed God in the worst way. I needed him in a way that I had not needed him before. I was in this place where unless I got in touch with him, I felt like I would dry up and die. This was the place I now found myself. But the good news was that Christ was passing by! Christ was in the neighborhood, I could see him at a distance, I could hear his voice, I could smell his fragrance, I could reach out and touch him if I pressed in a little harder. My help was near. On the ride back home, that evening I told Elleanor we had to go to his service on Sunday to see if what I had just experienced was real. I told her if Pastor Moore was not at church on Sunday and no one could attest to his whereabouts, I would know that he had been translated and taken away from this earth.

The name of Pastor Moore's church was Life Center Ministries, and their motto was "Where Healing Begins." It did not take me long to connect the dots and realize God was speaking. Both Charlotte ministries I had connected with had the word "Life" in their names. Both churches' motto was, "where healing begins." Yes, God had set me up for this encounter. He had placed me in a position where I had to make an intentional decision. Either I was going to accept him moving "outside of my traditional religious box" and embrace his mandate on my life through Life Center and Pastor Moore, or I was going to "miss" God altogether and become contented with what I knew him to be. The trouble with that was what I knew God to be in years past, he no longer was. During my spiritual journey with him, he had evolved into someone much more than I had come to know in times past. I was living in a past recollection of who he was when he had been changing and transitioning all the time. I thought I knew God but that was on such a limited and outdated basis. The side that Pastor Moore preached about was a side that I had heard of through the testimonies of people like my grandmother. I recall moments in the past when I got to this place and saw God's glory revealed. But nobody ever taught me how to go beyond the veil. No one ever showed me how to leave the outer court, go past the inner court and enter the Holy of Holies. They preached about it, they sang about it, and they taught Sunday School lessons about it, but I had only been beyond the veil on a few occasions. This man, this Methodist preacher, this man who was a few years younger than I, would become the catalyst that God would use to teach me how to go beyond the veil. I knew he had something I did not have. He possessed something I needed and wanted but at that moment, I could not fully articulate it. I made up in my mind that whatever it was that he had, I was going after it.

After hearing him speak that next Sunday and Thursday, I dared to execute one last cry. I took Elleanor by the hand after bible study on Thursday night and walked down the aisle to meet our purpose. We did not fully know what to expect of God, but we knew he had preserved our lives for "such a time as this." I knew that the road we had taken from New Orleans to Houston, back to New Orleans, and finally to Charlotte would ultimately be a "good place." When we shook Pastor Moore's hand, it was as if the weight of the world had lifted from off our shoulders. As he shook my hand and finally embraced me, no one sitting in the audience really knew what was taking place. This embrace felt as if I was being welcomed back home. But this had never been home for me, yet we knew it was the place for us. It was not the home of religion or denomination that I had known all my life. This home was a place of being in a true "relationship" with God. This embrace enveloped me in a way that allowed me to let go of all my inhibitions, my fears, my shortcomings, and failures. This encounter ushered me into *Eternity*. As for Elleanor, well she absolutely lost it and went forth in a dance. We just about started church all over again. She also realized we had finally made it "HOME."

I am not going to tell you what being home feels like, but everyone knows that feeling when you are truly at home. I will tell you a couple of very important things I came to appreciate as a result of finding a place I called home for a season. For one, I came to appreciate being in the process. I was in a process all my life and did not recognize it until just a couple of years ago. Most of the time I prayed to get out of the process, not understanding then, that going through the process was part of God's will for my life. I was too busy begging God to "move the mountain," that I never stopped to "count it all joy." Pastor Moore taught me about learning how to celebrate the process, the people, and the conditions that are part of the experience. Instead of getting mad at your enemies, Pastor Moore would say, "send them a bouquet of roses instead and tell them thank you." I spoke earlier in the book about being in the process of becoming. But what I did not share with you at that time was how the Lord has given Pastor Moore and Life Center Ministries the spirit of unconditional love, compassion, and acceptance. This is a ministry that, like New Life, will accept anybody. Most ministries say they will, but then give you glaring stares or a cold shoulder once you join. Jesus declared that those who were whole did not need a physician. Christ's mandate is to those that are sick, afflicted, and in need of a Savior. Pastor Moore, who later became Overseer and finally Bishop Moore, understood that all of us, and I do mean all of us, came to God as a mess! And for many of us, we continue to be a mess-in-progress. And although most people see you as you presently are, God sees you in your destined place, the place of your "shall be." The differences between the two are worlds apart. Bishop Moore was graced with the anointing to capture the very moment where one was and somehow take him to his place of "shall be." In doing so, he was able to impart the kind of hope needed to sustain you in the season of your becoming. This process is not pretty, but it guarantees to "beautify the meek with salvation." This process is not brief, but we are encouraged to "be not weary in well doing…for in due season, we shall reap if we faint not." The process can be mind-blowing at times, but God said he would keep those "in perfect peace whose mind is stayed on him."

One of the things I subconsciously accepted from religion was the lack of outward compassion toward others. This perspective resembled the Law of Moses in some respects. A former pastor of mine instructed me to "never teach weakness to the people." Though I agree with that statement in principle, it was the context of what he meant that later produced grave concerns for me in ministry and life. What I interpreted him as saying was that you should teach people that they are to be perfect, without blemish, and never mess up. He felt if you failed to preach this dogma, people would settle for less and fall short of reaching the "mark." Most people felt like they could never measure up to the Word of God and be this "perfect" Christian, so in many cases, people did not even try. Of if they tried and failed, they started pretending to be "holy" and learned how to keep sin and iniquity hidden and out of sight. We usually refer to this type of person as a hypocrite. The religious church put expectations and standards on people just like the Law did. We preached you onto a pedestal and exacted our "pound of flesh," if you failed. But if the truth is told, let us examine the ministry of Jesus for a second. Jesus chose twelve men to follow him. One was a curser, another a fighter, one a betrayer, one a doubter, one a tax collector who robbed his own people and one was a traitor. That amounts to 50% of the men he called had noticeable flaws. If Jesus were Director of Human Resources for many of our companies, he would have been fired for poor judgment in hiring staff. Jesus recognized our imperfections, and still, he loved us. This is what Bishop Moore instilled into those who became connected to Life Center Ministries.

The second thing I came to appreciate about this man and ministry was the freedom to be transparent. Most of us spend a lifetime "hiding" who we really are without ever becoming transparent to others. We are afraid to be truly transparent because when we do, we open ourselves up to others. It is at that moment that we become most vulnerable to men, but "open" to God. Let me tell you from first-hand experience this is not a comfortable feeling. Rather than being honest and transparent about ourselves and our walk with Christ, most of the preachers I heard growing up presented the "Superman" persona where they would preach the glory of Christ, and never mention the missteps they made along the way. I grew up thinking that members of the five-fold ministries were somewhat infallible. Most of us have become experts at the ability to erect barriers at the drop of a hat. Some of us have put up enough emotional walls that we could be licensed as brick masons. Being transparent is not a very pleasant emotional experience. But at the same time, being self-transparent can lead to the ultimate in freeing yourself from bondage. In the first instance, being transparent involves divulging your weaknesses or struggles to others. In this stage, we must seek God to direct us to one who is spiritual enough to carry the "weight" of what is said without judgment. I like to call this stage "Show and Tell." For it is here that we open up and *show, or reveal* our true selves to brothers and sisters. Here we *tell* them about our hearts in hopes that they can undergird us in a way that will edify and build us up. Sometimes we error in judgment and connect ourselves with people who cannot handle our "nakedness." Rather than cover us, they expose us to the world and our enemies. When we "uncover" ourselves to them, we sometimes find ourselves in a similar position as Noah. When Noah's son Ham found his father drunk inside his tent, he exposed his nakedness to others instead of covering him, as did Shem and Japheth. How many Hams have we exposed ourselves to, only to discover that what was said in confidence has now become Headline News! Well, if you are like me, it only takes one or two times to go through something like this before you shut down and cut yourself off from people. I have been there. This wall becomes your best friend. Naturally, the wall serves its purpose of not letting anyone in. But it also causes you to become hostage to your own identity. You become a captive to your own guilt. Satan is cunning enough to use any weapon, even guilt, to keep you hiding behind your mask. Religion has ruined many persons and will cause countless others to be lost, all for the sake of "saving face." You do not believe me? Just look at the altars in our churches. When the minister makes the appeal, who do we usually see at the altar? If we are fortunate, we may see sinners, backsliders and the unchurched come forth. But where are the saints? Where are our preachers, teachers, missionaries, deacons, mothers, and musicians? We can usually be found at the altar but on the wrong side of the altar. Rather than in a position of ministering, we should be the ones coming to be ministered to. But why do we not see this phenomenon frequently? Why are we not at the altar crying out? Is brokenness reserved only for the sinner? The reason church members are not crowding the alter is that we wish to remain hidden behind our masks so others, "the church," will not know! We have hidden behind and worn our church masks for so long, that we have forgotten what the real "us" looks like. The visible mask which we wear to church, the one everyone sees, is not us. It is the image of you that you feel comfortable enough to reveal to others. You want them to see the image of some Superhero leaping tall buildings in a single bound. It is "The You," that you have rehearsed and staged all these years. It is the counterfeit you who is always together, always "cool, calm and collected." It is the fake you that people have come to expect. After all, you do have a position and reputation to protect and what would people say if they observed you coming for prayer? So, when the altar call is made, you sense the Spirit of the Lord urging you to step out and go to the altar. But you resist and talk yourself into believing that "I will stand at my seat and utter my prayer silently unto the Lord." And we miss the opportunity time and time again to bring ourselves to the altar where the issue that we struggle with can be put to death publicly!

At Life Center, I learned it was not about the mask. It was really about YOU! God knows YOU and he wants fellowship with the person hiding behind the mask. It is not until you pull the mask off and allow yourself to become transparent to God and others, that real transformation takes place. This is when God is at his best when you come to him broken. Life Center is where I discovered how to remove my mask. I learned the mask represents different things to different people and everyone is not affected the same way. For me, the vehicle that helped me to remove my mask was WORSHIP. When I discovered pure unadulterated worship, I found the key to getting into God's presence. Religion taught me to seek God's hand, worship taught me to seek his face. When I worship, I lose all prohibitions and inhibitions about who I am, my position and title, and what people think of me. Worship taught me how to "get into" the very presence of God. I found a place where I could remove the mask and care less about being judged for who I was or what position I held within the church. The ministry fostered such an anointing, that when I found myself in worship, others around me joined in with my celebration, understanding that I was being set free from something. Instead of judging me, they celebrated the work the Spirit was performing in me. Worship exposed me for the wretch that I was and caused me to rejoice over the redeeming work of Christ. Worship brought me from *where I was* to <u>where I am</u>. Worship took me from the *"use to be"* and set me down in the "shall be" of God. Worship shined a light inside of my soul that caused me to confront things that I knew about myself but did not want to face. Worship gave me the strength to conquer and overcome challenges in my life. In worship, I was able to hear God in a way I never had before. I got so close to the Lord in worship, I could hear him whisper. Worship helped me to shut out all the distractions and focus only on the one that mattered, God. Worship took me from where I was to where I needed to be. Worship transcended me from earth to glory and put me in a place where God revealed himself to me as the "I AM." Religion did not and could not do this for me. Worship did. Religion took me to levels, while worship took me to dimensions. Religion bound me, but worship set me free. Religion gave me sight, but worship gave me faith. Religion birthed in me a **denomination**, but worship birthed in me a **relationship**. I can recall on at least two occasions where the worship became so intense, that I saw the angels of the Lord moving about in the upper chambers of the sanctuary. It reminded me of the small church where I first gave my life to Jesus and to see the room literally filled with smoke, which I now know was the glory of God. As a part of COGIC, I have been to many convocations, gatherings, and meetings where the Lord would make an appearance. But there were many more times when it was "church as usual." You pay your report, hear a few good songs, get a shout, hear a good message, raise an offering, and go home. But to this day, I have never been associated with a body of believers such as Life Center Fellowship Ministries where every time we gathered as a fellowship, God did not fail to dwell among us. And when I say dwell, I mean every meeting was "God Anointed," where devils were cast out, people delivered, sick healed, backsliders reclaimed, sinners saved, and people would still be on the floor hours after the benediction had been given. My two daughters often relate the moving of the Holy Spirit to a visual of Jesus riding down the street on a moped. When we just have church somewhere, they will remark that "Jesus passed by and did not even get off of his moped." But when we experienced a "visitation" of the holy spirit they would say, "Jesus got off his moped, took his helmet off, and came and sat down in the church." That is the way Life Center Fellowship Ministry gatherings were, Jesus never once failed to join us whether we gathered in Charleston, Charlotte, Tallahassee, Greenville, Albany, Boiling Springs, Atlanta, or wherever we met. Jesus got off his moped and came on in.

CHAPTER 20

The Enemies Of Purpose

Now you might feel that at this point in my life, everything was set for me to "enter in." I had taken a journey, learned a lot about myself, and seemed to be on the brink of my breakthrough. But how many of you know that the enemy will not step aside and allow you to walk in purpose without doing all he can to stop you? If Satan can stop you from fulfilling the purpose that God created for you, he knows you will never reach your destiny. He is going to reach deep into his arsenal and throw everything he has at you to discourage, defeat, and destroy your path to fulfilling your purpose. He uses different tactics on different people, targeting areas of your life where you are most vulnerable. He never attacks you at the point of your strength but lies dormant until he sees a weakness exposed. Samson was the strongest human being to ever live, yet he was defeated by a physically weak female who used his weakness, lust, to entrap and enslave him.

For me, there were several areas, some of which I continue to battle, that came to keep me from purpose. The first enemy was fear. My fear came in capital letters – F E A R! The fear of failure, the fear of being wrong, the fear to step out and trust God, the fear to trust others, the fear of what others would say, the fear of how others perceived me, the fear of failing to make ends meet. You get the picture. I was just about afraid of everything. The Word of God declares that "fear has torment," and living in a constant state of fear is one of the worst experiences life has to offer. It was as if everything that could go wrong, did go wrong. It was a spiritual reaction that resulted in a true sense of the self-fulfilling prophecy. The self-fulfilling prophecy is the psychological phenomenon of someone "predicting" or expecting something, and this prediction or expectation comes true simply because one believes it will, and their resulting behaviors align to fulfill those beliefs. The Bible puts it this way, "as a man thinketh in his heart, so is he." It goes on to add, "Death and life are in the power of the tongue." Godly success becomes unattainable not because of a lack on the Lord's part but rather because we have planted the seeds of doubt so deeply into our inner spirit, that it becomes impossible to override both natural and spiritual laws God has established to govern our lives. This then becomes the primary reason our minds must be "transformed," according to Apostle Paul in the 12th chapter of the book of Romans.

I came to understand not many years ago that the fear I was feeling was birthed in me as a young child. As a child and adolescent, I had no fears about what I could accomplish in the secular world. I was a straight-A student, and although not a genius, I was gifted academically enough to graduate sixth in my graduating high school class. There was never any situation in school that I thought was too difficult for me. The church arena however was a different situation. Because I did not come from the leadership lineage that several of my peers came from,

I always felt like I was at a disadvantage. I did all the right things in the church, but when it came to important events or spotlight moments, sons and daughters of District Superintendents, District Missionaries or Jurisdictional Bishops always seemed to come out ahead of me. The best I had to offer in the way of legacy was my grandmother. She was one of the pioneers of The Church of God in Christ. Despite her anointing, she was elderly, uneducated, and not in the inner circle of the church elite. It appeared several of my peers who were less equipped than me, managed to get promoted before I did. This left an indelible wound in my spirit that caused me to doubt who I was in God. This small pebble of doubt grew and matured into a massive boulder of fear that I allowed, crippling my forward movement, and causing a detour in my fulfilling my assignment in the Kingdom.

This fear crippled me to the extent that it created barriers in my life which led to challenges in my finances, my ministry, my spiritual growth, my marriage, and my family. Many times, I can remember hearing the voice of God instructing me to "step out on faith." Because I allowed doubt and fear to take residence in my heart, I found myself paralyzed and failed to move on to what God had spoken. I found myself overanalyzing everything and hiding behind excuses. Reflecting over the many years in ministry, I realized it was my lack of faith that placed me years behind in fulfilling my purpose. I should have been…I could have been…I would have been, are all epitaphs of the greatness that God was trying to release in me over the years. I acknowledge I was the one who allowed the enemy to plant little seeds of fear inside of me which grew and blocked my faith in trusting God.

By nature, I consider myself to be an analytical person. By that I mean I have always tried to figure God out through my intellect. How many of you know you will never be able to comprehend or figure God out? I always found myself attempting to figure things out and "see" what God was doing in my life. As much as I tried to know him in my intellect, I continued to miss him in my heart and spirit. To move with God, you must do so not with what you see but rather, with what you know. Faith is moving on what you believe and not what you see. And this "knowing" has nothing to do with your intelligence. Romans 8:28 states, "and we know that all things work together for good to them that love God, to them who are the called according to his purpose." This knowing has everything to do with your trust in the person who spoke the promise. Either you will trust God for what you know of his character, or you will depend on your resources to sustain and direct you. I was too busy looking at myself for the answer and not God. With a concept like that, no wonder I was taking one step forward and five steps backward. My lack of faith led to direct disobedience to God in the Tithe. Many times, I came face-to-face with a decision to tithe or not to tithe. I always reasoned that I just could not afford to tithe. The reality was I could not afford, not to tithe. Yes, I knew tithing was right. Everyone preached it, taught it, and some practiced it. But I still disobeyed it. I always was able to justify a reason for not tithing. I had to take care of my family, the car broke down, I needed to purchase food for the house, and so on and so on. I would always fall back on the scripture 1 Timothy 5:8, which I had heard taught all my life, "if any provide not for his own, and especially for those of his own house, he had denied the faith, and is "worse than an infidel." And of course, God would not want me to fall into that category I would reason, so I would use the tithe on everything but what God originally intended it to be used for. And as the years went by, it became harder and harder for me to break this stronghold in my life.

Another enemy of purpose became the "busyness of ministry." I found myself always engaged in doing the work of the ministry never realizing I was neglecting the Lord of the Work. Have you ever gotten so caught up in working in ministry that you found yourself almost in a robotic-like fashion going through the motions? It was as if everyone was pulling on me for something. I need you over here for marriage counseling, no, over here for a preached Word. You are needed here for a men's retreat, how about ministering to a youth in crisis? I mean I worked in the Sunday school department, Youth People Willing Workers, sang in the choir, served as Youth Pastor, Evangelism President, and even served in the local and Jurisdictional Auxiliaries in Ministry Chairman. All of this besides serving as senior pastor to three churches in three different states at one time or another. This became repetitive and redundant to the extent that I was working in ministry all the time but not allowing

God to minister to me. Because of past religious training, I had been taught to always be a good soldier and follow orders. One day a friend of mine from Charleston, South Carolina spoke to me words I will never forget. She said she had been pulled in so many directions at once trying to fulfill the desires of her leader that she recognized she was not being effective in any area. Ultimately, she had to inform the leader that she would not be able to accept certain assignments he had in mind for her to do. I asked the question, "How did you say no to your leader?" She replied, "I simply put an N and an O together and said "NO!" As simple as that sounded until I heard her say that, I had no clue as to how to say NO. Many Christians find themselves working all over the place and not seeing effective and lasting results anywhere. Most times we start out working in areas not because of a specific anointing in that area, but out of necessity due to the shortage of physical manpower in the church or a certain skill set or expertise, you may possess. The danger in doing this is sometimes we convince ourselves to believe that because we experienced a measure of success in this area, this has to be the place where God has called us to. But I believe that when God sees our hearts and he sees us willing to pitch in and help wherever we are asked, he blesses us and helps to bring about positive results. But I also believe this is only for a season. Afterward, God will send someone else into the ministry who IS anointed and gifted to take on the task we had been doing and to do it more effectively than we did. But by then, many of us feel like we have become an "expert" in this area, and no one can do it better than us. After all, we have been successful in the past and we have heard praise from others who celebrated our achievements. The crazy thing is that the body is still being blessed, not because of us but because God is faithful to his WORD. Meantime, we are missing it BIG TIME, because we have lost our "soul-connection" to the Lord. So, we spend an inordinate amount of time being busy with ministry, but not busy doing real ministry. One of the major flaws with this entire premise I later learned is that leaders are slow to begin training and grooming successors to replace them when the time comes. Instead of prayerfully seeking out those to "pass the torch" to, we wait and hold onto whatever title or position for as long as we can. By the time it becomes evident a successor is needed, we are either too old, in poor physical health, have missed valuable time with our spouses and children, and have missed opportunity after opportunity to successfully mentor and "pour into" the next person designated to lead. It happens on every level and in every position. It saddens me when I hear of someone unable to function in their role and capacity but still is allowed to maintain the position simply out of loyalty, greed, or a combination of both. I always thought what a magnanimous and unselfish gesture to see a leader step aside and pass the torch onto an up-and-coming individual whom the Lord has laid his hand upon. Unfortunately, what I have witnessed too many times is we wait until the person is senile, can hardly get around, is disabled, and is way past their prime of being an effective leader before any action is taken to replace that individual. Do we throw away people who have given their lives to ministry now that they have passed their prime? Definitely not! But think about the value of having such a person in the role of an advisor or Emeritus designee who will still be celebrated for the contributions they have made to the body of Christ.

Our activity working with ministry oftentimes prohibits us from being sensitive to the voice of God. Have you ever noticed God seldom yells to get our attention? In the hustle and bustle of the day's activities, if you can calm yourself down, you can usually hear God talking. I heard someone once say, "It ain't that God is not talking...it is that we're not listening." God will not compete with our attention span by trying to be the loudest, most boisterous, or overbearing force. Instead, he chooses to wait until the brouhaha and hoopla subside and then he whispers what he wants to say to our spirit man. The challenge we have is that we have been battling all day with voices that have been loud, boisterous, and overbearing, not to exclude obnoxious, irritating, and vexing. By the time God speaks to us unless he is speaking through a megaphone or loudspeaker, he has no chance of getting our attention. Not only have we gone brain-dead, but more importantly we have gone spirit-dead, in the sense that we have unconsciously shut down our inner man. So, God is talking, but guess what, nobody is home, and no one is listening. And it is a sad thing when we become more familiar with the voice of the Bishop or Overseer, Pastor or Minister, Prophet or Teacher, Mother or Covenant Partner more than we are with the voice of our Lord and Savior. It is sad when we anticipate the beck and call of man and yet fail to hear God's pleadings. It is an indictment of our walk with the Lord when we are attuned to what our spiritual leaders' desires are because we have spent so much time in their presence yet have no clue as to what direction the Lord would have us go. We are really messed up when we can repeat verbatim what the leadership of the church mandates are, while unable to articulate what the "will of the Lord is" for the people of God or even ourselves.

Hearing the voice of man and not God leads us to another enemy of purpose and that is, needing the approval of man to move in what God has already spoken. Yes, there are times when God speaks but it is not quite time to move. Remember God anointed David as King but sent him back to tending his father's sheep until his season came due? But even in those "seasons", it becomes a time of preparation and apprenticeship where we cultivate the gifts that we will need to fulfill our assignment. Contrary to this time of development, we usually spend our time being "groomed" by leadership to perpetuate our weaknesses and shortcomings. Instead of this being a season in which we become familiar with God's voice, this time becomes a period of indoctrination to the "system" we call a denomination. And in the process of being groomed, trained, and prepped for the denomination, we usually fall prey to needing to be validated by someone. This innate need to be validated by someone, causes us to become dependent on man, and not God, as our source. Consequently, the ability to validate another's calling, anointing, and giftings usually affords the person with this level of authority and opportunity to "play God" and determine our path up or down the ladder of churchdom. This is a dangerous trap because it ushers in the intervention of man with his inherent flaws. We wind up spending precious time trying to impress others in a significant way. If we are not careful subconsciously or not, we may find ourselves manipulating the Spirit in such a way as to put ourselves in a favorable position or light. I remember when I pastored a ministry in another state, one of the senior sisters in our ministry approached me with a proposal. She suggested appointing a certain brother as a deacon and placing him over the finances of the ministry. Because he had a good job and was making a lot of money, she guaranteed that our offerings would increase significantly. Having a small struggling church at the time, the thought crossed my mind for a very brief second. I then found myself rebuking the sister and admonishing every member that, promotion from God is not based on what you can do for him, but rather on what he finds you doing before being called. And before any thoughts of promotion for this brother, I had already observed him "boastfully" putting in a dollar or two and at times, even amounts as small as loose silver change. I went on to comment that whether we collected 5 cents in offerings or $1,000.00, the integrity of the ministry could not be bought or sold, nor could I be bribed for any amount of money. That brother soon left the ministry and the sister who recommended him for the position was discovered dead in her own home.

Needing the approval of others always empowers man in a way God never intended. If this were the case then God would be investing your purpose in the hands of shortsighted, greed-influenced, power-hungry, and disease-infected mankind. And how many of you are willing to trust the "final answer" to someone with these issues? Following the program of others when God has spoken to you concerning your purpose is never a wise thing to do. But we often find ourselves in similar situations as we strive to please a man in the form of service. There is always a single Vision for the corporate house that rests with the specific leader of the ministry. But that vision never negates the divine purpose and assignment of the individual believer. God is a God of Order and is wise enough to assign certain individuals to certain ministries and leaders that will complement, rather than repel each other. But when we fail to hear from God, we are more than likely to confuse, misunderstand, or misinterpret our assignment and walk in our own knowledge. And God tells us in Proverbs 3:5-6, "and lean not unto thine own understanding, in all thy ways acknowledge him, and he shall direct thy paths." But there are times when we go along, to get along. We buckle under the pressures of conformity and seek to assimilate God's agenda into the agenda of the leader or majority. This is normally referred to as not, "rocking the boat."

Religion speaks to conformity. Religion says to fit in, be accepted, join the boys, and become part of the family. Religion is the hallmark of "sameness." But God is calling us to be "transformed by the renewing of our minds." Every great movement in history called for a transformation of some sort to be made. And that transformation usually began with one man. One man who was brave enough to buck the status quo; one person radical enough to challenge the tradition of the fathers; one soul courageous enough to stand in the face of insurmountable odds; one voice strong enough to overpower the whispers of defeat; one heart big enough to expand its compassion beyond its borders and one vision bold enough to strive for excellence in a sea of mediocrity.

Throughout the echoes of time, God has always asked for a man. In the book of Isaiah 6:8, the Lord asks the question, "Whom shall I send, and who will go for us?" This has been an age-old question asked by the Godhead. And throughout the annuals of time, someone has stepped up, as unworthy as they were, and answered the call. "Here am I, send me," has been the reply from Abram to Noah, from Moses to Samuel, from Ester to David, from Isaiah to Daniel, from Jesus to Paul, and from those heroes of faith to you and I today.

Today I stand ready, willing, and finally able to accomplish all that God has assigned to my hands. Despite every trial, every struggle, every failure, every proclivity, and every weakness, I am ready, available, and willing to be used by God to fulfill his purpose with my life. It is not until we recognize our weakness that God's strength can be perfected in us. I had to learn that to walk in purpose and fulfill destiny, I had to come to grips with my own anointing and calling. I also had to acknowledge my fears, failures, and flaws. Although I tried to find myself in so many others, I discovered later in my life that like David, I could not go to war with another man's armor. It just would not fit no matter how it was tailored. Their anointing was for them and their day. The anointing God has reserved for me is meant only for me. No one else wears it, uses it, duplicates it, or carbon copies it. It has been so masterfully crafted by God himself, that his anointing in my life is designed to work with my personality, my sense of style, my humanity, and my spirit.

Believe me when I tell you that you are destined for greatness in the kingdom and only you can prevent that from happening. The devil cannot stop you; your mother cannot stop you; your friends cannot stop you; your pastor cannot stop you, and your church cannot stop you. As I journey along, I continue to discover places in God I never knew existed. Each level of relationship I discover with God brings me closer to my ultimate destiny and that is to become so consumed with God's presence, that whenever anyone looks at me, all they see is the glory of God. For when men truly see the glory of the only true and living God, it WILL forever change their lives and transcend them from mortality to immortality. It will take them from a place of guilt to a place of justification. And make no mistake about it, men will not be eternally changed until they have experienced God's Glory. Can't no book, no song, no seminar, no conference, no concept, no invention, and no individual bring about Eternal

Change like an encounter with the Lord Jesus Christ. I am not talking about a shout or dance, speaking in tongues, running around the church, or even speaking prophetic words over someone. How do I know? It was not until I tapped into his very glory that the manifestation of my own life changed. In eternity, God knew that I had already changed. But it was not until I was able to move from Tradition to Relationship that God truly revealed himself to me. And now I have moved to a place in him where my Relationship has overwhelmed my tradition and brought me to a place of fulfillment and destiny in him. I pray that somehow this vehicle helps you to also find your place in him.

Your Journey Starts Now...

About The Author

Pastor George R. Montgomery, Sr

Pastor George R. Montgomery is a native of New Orleans, Louisiana. With over 54 years in Kingdom ministry, he remains committed to a life of integrity, sanctification, and godly living. Having served as Senior Pastor of Houma Church of God In Christ, in Houma, La., Evangelist Temple Church of God in Christ, in Bay City, Texas and Life Center Ministries, Greensboro, North Carolina, Pastor Montgomery continues to provide spiritual mentorship and support to various pastors and ministries across the United States.

Pastor Montgomery received his undergraduate degree from Tulane University in New Orleans in 1980 and furthered his theological studies at the C.H. Mason Bible

College in Houston, Texas. He has served on the faculty of The Greater New Orleans Bible Institute, in New Orleans, Louisiana and The Life Center Training Institute in Charlotte, North Carolina. Part of his ministerial service has included being Jurisdictional Chairman of the Auxiliaries In Ministry (AIM) Convention for the Louisiana Ecclesiastical Second Jurisdiction of the Church of God In Christ and Chairman of the Board of Presbyters for Life Center Ministries Fellowship of Churches.

He has been involved for more than 33 years in the fields of Case Management, Community Support, Wraparound Services, Systems of Care, Therapeutic Foster Care, and Child Welfare. His work has included educating several counties across the country in mental health, behavioral disorders, and trauma-focused strategies. He currently serves as the Foster Care Licensing Social Worker for Rowan County Department of Social Services, in Salisbury, North Carolina.

Blessed to be married to Lady Elleanor Gray Montgomery for 41 years and father of Keosha, Courtney, and George Montgomery Jr, together they have promoted the gospel through their ministry to encourage, build, restore, inspire, and empower the Body of Christ.

www.ingramcontent.com/pod-product-compliance
Lightning Source LLC
LaVergne TN
LVHW061035070526
838201LV00073B/5040